Winning
Horse Racing
Formulae

D1634347

Winning Horse Racing Formulae

David Duncan

foulsham
LONDON • NEW YORK • TORONTO • SYDNEY

foulsham

The Publishing House, Bennetts Close,
Cippenham, Berkshire, SL1 5AP, England.

ISBN 0-572-02425-8

Printed in Great Britain by Cox & Wyman Ltd, Reading, Berks

CONTENTS

✳

INTRODUCTION

The definitive guide to betting on horses has never been written, and in all probability never will be. The sport of racing thoroughbreds in Britain is so complex and so diverse that over any reasonable period of time the results of races cannot be predicted with a sufficient degree of accuracy to guarantee consistent profits for even the most knowledgeable of backers. In addition, with the experience of over a century-and-a-half of organised betting behind them, the bookmakers of today are so professional in their approach to odds-making for a multi-million pound industry, that the punter, however skilled, will always be at something of a disadvantage.

All that said, I believe it is no idle boast to claim that this book is the most comprehensive treatise on racing and betting that has ever appeared in print. My intimate association with the sport goes back nearly 40 years, so I can examine every aspect of it from a betting point of view and I hope I have communicated it in a clear and concise way that beginners as well as seasoned enthusiasts will find easy to follow. This in-depth analysis is designed to help the reader get the best from a pastime which will obviously be more pleasurable if they can contrive a profit from it.

Beginning with single selections, the first half of the book is devoted to the difficult and controversial subject of staking correctly, and incorporates an appreciation of the much-vaunted concept of 'value' in relation to chance. It then moves from level stakes to sophisticated methods of regulating them in such a way as to maximise the potential for financial gain. There are chapters on racing permutations for single selections and on ways of combining bets on more than one horse in a race, either to increase the possibility of a really big win from multiple selections or to achieve steadier profits by making a punters' 'book' against the bookmakers in order to beat them at their own game.

I look at selection procedures too in great detail, backed up by statistics providing readers with valuable knowledge unavailable elsewhere, as well as expertise, much of which they could probably never hope to acquire by trial and error. There is also a section giving complete details of a number of fully automatic racing systems which have been tried and tested over many years and which have the potential to win again in the seasons to come.

My tour through the betting jungle concludes with a discussion of overall betting strategy, supported by a set of indicators that will nearly always point in the right direction in a given set of circumstances and, almost as important, steer the unwary away from the many pitfalls which lie in wait for anyone who bets on horses.

It is never possible to remove the element of gambling from the sport entirely, and no one would want that to happen. There is, of course, no such thing as a racing certainty, and no certain way of making a betting profit from racing. For this reason no one should ever stake more than they can reasonably afford to lose on their opinions about horse-racing contests, whether independently formed or arrived at by following the advice given in these pages.

Traditionally, racing, and betting in particular, have been seen as male preserves. In fact this was never entirely the case and nowadays it is definitely not so. Women are involved at all levels in every racing activity; this includes the very large numbers of female punters who try to make their betting pay as a way of enhancing their interest in the sport. This book, therefore, is addressed to them as much as to men, and is written in the belief that all will find it equally instructive and hopefully profitable when it comes to their betting forays either against the bookmakers or on the Tote.

David Duncan

1

Stake Right, Lose Less and Win More

Variable Stakes – The Pitfalls

A well-known professional gambler once remarked that it is not how many winners you back that counts in the end, but how you stake on them. If you think about it this must be right, for unless the punter's strike rate of winners is so low as to be virtually hopeless in the long term, the chance of a profit will always be determined by what is bet on successful nominations in relation to the stakes on losers.

This is a truism that has probably not occurred to a lot of punters, however long they have been at the game. Take for example this rota of bets:

Four Horses: £10 staked.

£4	6–4	Lost
£5	7–2	Lost
50p	7–1	Won
50p	7–1	Won

For whatever reason, the backer has decided that his strongest preference among the four horses is for the one at the second-best odds. But what is the outcome? For his total outlay of £10 he receives only £8 before tax in return, a LOSS of £2 overall.

Yet if the £10 stake had been divided equally between the four horses, there would have been a PROFIT of no less than £30 before tax! Incredible, but bookmakers receive bets like these in large quantities every racing day.

Does this mean that level stakes is always the best? Not necessarily, although it must be said right from the start that it will always be the safest method of staking for any punter, big or small, to adopt. And this is for the simple reason that having the same amount on each selection is a sure way of avoiding the catastrophic mishit mirrored in the above example. With an equal distribution on each selection of the total amount bet over a given period, at least the backer receives full credit for the winners he backs, even if he has to accept that all his losers will have the same weight in the final reckoning.

The problem with level stakes, especially from the point of view of the ordinary punter betting in relatively small amounts, is that in racing it can be very difficult to build up a reasonable gain, even over a lengthy period. Take someone who is regularly able to find say, 40 per cent of winners from all the horses backed, but at an average price of only 6–4. This will do no better than break even overall, and with betting tax will actually lose, despite a very respectable score of winning selections.

Finding a way out of this conundrum is a huge problem. Either the backer must somehow increase the ratio of winners to losers, with the risk of a reduction in the average starting price, or must back horses at better prices, thereby risking a drop in the percentage of winners. An attempt to strike the right balance could easily upset the apple cart which would result in doing worse than before.

The other problem with level stakes is one of betting psychology as much as anything. Since they offer neither a quick road to profit nor an easy escape route when things go wrong, they are not very exciting. Turning a successful run into a spectacular gain, assuming the run is continued, is always going to be a lengthy process. Equally, once a losing run sets in, there is bound to be a long, hard road back from the financial red to black, even if the number of winners improves dramatically.

Little wonder therefore that most punters, even if they accept the general notion of staking roughly the same on each horse in line with their betting means, still like to vary the amounts of their bets according to the strength of their convictions about this or that selection.

Let us take another example of variable staking on a series of bets covering four horses. In this case there is a strong possibility that the backer has allowed his stakes to be determined by the prices of his selections rather than by his own judgement of relative chances.

Four Horses: £10 staked.

£5	6–4	Lost
£3	7–2	Lost
£1.50	8–1	Lost
50p	10–1	Won

This time there were three losers offset by a 10–1 winner, yielding an overall, pre-tax LOSS of £4.50. However, had the £10 been split equally between the four horses with bets of £2.50 on each, the outcome would have been a PROFIT of £17.50 before tax. Not quite the debacle of the first example, but bad enough.

No doubt anyone making this wager would argue in their own defence, after the event at least, that they fancied the 6–4 shot much more than the rest, hence the large stake on that animal. This is all very well if the selection criteria, whatever they might have been, had genuinely indicated that the horse at 6–4 was indeed the best bet, and that the others had lesser chances commensurate with the amount bet on them. For many punters it is much more likely that the stakes were fixed, not by any objective measure of relative chance but, solely according to the probable odds for each, with the bigger stakes on the shorter prices.

Value in Betting – The Illusion

This belief that the 'market', whether on the racecourse or in the shape of a newspaper betting forecast, will nearly always be right, colours the thinking behind many people's attitude to staking. To rid the mind of this conviction is certainly not easy, and this brings us to the concept of 'value' which embraces a different and, in some ways, opposite view of how the betting market should determine stakes.

Value is the buzz word among the betting fraternity in the 1990s. Anyone who consistently finds value in the odds of the horses backed, we are told, must have a better chance of winning over a period of time than someone who is content to accept any old price about a fancied animal.

This is all very well, but how is value to be assessed? Racing is an 'opinion' sport when it comes to betting, and whether or not the price about a particular runner represents something-for-nothing is just as much a matter of opinion as the wide variety of views different people will frequently take over the possible outcome of a given race. No one has yet discovered an accurate measure of odds in relation to true chance or, if they have, they are keeping it to themselves and for very good reasons. Plenty of theories have been aired, for which big claims have been made, but in practice, in the hard world of the modern betting industry value is an elusive, perhaps even an illusory concept. Everyone wants to back a true 3–1 chance at 8–1 but this is rarely possible. Professional bookmakers and odds-makers are just not in the business of making mistakes of this kind.

This fact is well illustrated if practically any horse race is analysed according to the method of converting odds to percentages used by the bookmakers themselves in framing the odds for races. Just one example at this point will serve to make the realities of the situation clear.

Below are the runners and prices for a recent renewal of the season's fifth and final Classic, the St Leger run at Doncaster in September. There were 11 horses in the field, so each of them had a mathematical 10–1 chance of winning, and this is shown immediately to the right of the names of the runners, but expressed as a percentage:

$100 \div (10 + 1) = 9.1$ per cent to the nearest 0.1 per cent.

The next column shows the actual price of each horse similarly converted to a percentage, for example:

Dushyantor at 2–1; $100 \div (2 + 1) = 33.3$ per cent.

The last two columns reveal by how much the available odds differ in percentage terms from the real mathematical chance, either to the bookmakers' or the backer's advantage as the case may be. With Dushyantor the real odds are 10–1 against in purely mathematical terms, but the bookmaker offers only 2–1, a 24.2 per cent advantage in his favour.

On the other hand, with Flying Legend at 18–1, the backer has the advantage this time, one of 3.8 per cent which represents the difference between the available odds and the real chance of 10–1.

In a race which, given the shape of the market, the bookmakers definitely expected Dushyantor to win (he was beaten a neck by Shantou), clearly all the value lies not with the backers but with the bookmaker. Only about half the field had any real chance of succeeding, and in five cases the odds are in his favour. The odds of Heron Island give no advantage either way, but the punters are left with the 'edge' just for the 'rags' which could only win in the event of a major, virtually unpredictable, form upset. In other words, if the layers' assessment of the race is no better than approximately correct, the market has been

Odds	Horse	Mathematical probability %	Odds converted to probability %	Bookmakers' advantage %	Backer's advantage %
2–1	DUSHYANTOR	9.1	33.3	24.2	
5–1	MONS	9.1	16.7	7.6	
7–1	GORDI	9.1	12.5	3.4	
8–1	SHANTOU	9.1	11.1	2.0	
8–1	ST MAWES	9.1	11.1	2.0	
10–1	HERON ISLAND	9.1	9.1	Nil	
11–1	SHARAF KABEER	9.1	8.3		0.8
16–1	WILAWANDER	9.1	5.9		3.2
18–1	FLYING LEGEND	9.1	5.3		3.8
28–1	SAMRAAN	9.1	3.4		5.7
50–1	DESERT BOY	9.1	2.0		7.1
		100.1	118.7 −100.1	39.2 −20.6	20.6
			Over-round = 18.6	18.6	

Note: the 'over-round' advantage of 100.1 per cent to the bookmakers on the race as a whole is due to the rounding up or down of percentages to the nearest 0.1 per cent.

framed in such a way that there is no value anywhere for the backer.

It is a sad fact of betting life that the above scenario is typical of the betting market on the vast majority of races, day in, day out, week in, week out. Only when a runner has been seriously underestimated, which happens rarely, does the informed or inspired backer have the opportunity to apply the concept of value profitably.

All this shows just what the backer is up against in his search for a profit. It is very difficult to nullify, let alone reverse, the bookmakers' trading margin on any race, but there is one simple measure which sensible punters can take to protect themselves to some extent. This is to bet only in relatively small fields. A glance at the two races for which the full rota of odds are set out below should be enough to hammer home this vital point. Both events took place on the same day at a Glorious Goodwood meeting.

STEWARDS' CUP

Odds	Horse	Odds converted to probability %
7–1	HUMBERT'S LANDING	12.5
15–2	DUPLICITY	11.8
8–1	POKER CHIP	11.1
12–1	AGWA	7.7
14–1	HOW'S YER FATHER	6.7
14–1	COOL JAZZ	6.7
14–1	MARGARET'S GIFT	6.7
14–1	PETULA	6.7
16–1	VENTURE CAPITALIST	5.9
16–1	MISTER JOLSON	5.9
16–1	FOR THE PRESENT	5.9
20–1	DOUBLE BLUE	4.8
20–1	LAW COMMISSION	4.8
20–1	LORD OLIVIER	4.8
20–1	JATO	4.8
20–1	MASTER PLANNER	4.8
25–1	DARK EYED LADY	3.8
33–1	GORINSKY	2.9
33–1	BALLASECRET	2.9
33–1	BAROSSA VALLEY	2.9
50–1	SAMSOLOM	2.0
66–1	MASTER OF PASSION	1.5
66–1	BELLS OF LONGWICK	1.5
100–1	GREEN'S BID	1.0
100–1	VILLAGE GREEN	1.0
100–1	ORTHORHOMBUS	1.0
		132.1

Odds	Horse	Odds converted to probability %
6–4	PHARAMINEUX	40.0
3–1	ISLE OF PEARLS	25.0
7–2	ALCOVE	22.2
13–2	AMANCIO	13.3
10–1	MELLABY	9.1
		109.6

A comparison of the over-round in these two races reveals the trap which the bookmakers habitually lay for inexperienced punters, as well as informed ones whose knowledge of betting mathematics is not always all it should be. Although all the odds for the Stewards' Cup, a very big handicap with many runners, look generous, both in terms of prices for individual contenders and as a whole, in fact they are no such thing. The over-round on the race is as high as 32.1 per cent. In the small-field race on the other hand, layers competing for business in the Ring have been unable to hide their lack of generosity behind a big field with lots of fancied candidates. In this race their margin is as low as 9.6 per cent, a huge difference compared with 32.1 per cent.

Generally speaking, two per cent for each runner in a race will aggregate to the over-round to which bookmakers can be expected to bet, up to a maximum of about 35 per cent. In small fields, therefore, there is much greater value for the punter. Apparently 'tasty' prices in races with a lot of runners, especially handicaps, are a snare and a delusion. Apart from serious errors by the bookmakers which are as scarce as taxis on a wet night, without exception every runner in a small field offers better value, whatever its price. Beyond that, this author would not care to speculate when it comes to trying to establish a value system by which the price on offer for a horse can be compared to its real chance on form.

Others have tried and failed. Modern British ideas about value are similar to the long-standing American concept of 'overlays' which attempt, by an independent assessment of chances, to discover in *pari-mutuel* pools, horses standing at odds significantly better than a price which would reflect their true prospect of winning.

There are no legal bookmakers in the USA. So with overlays the theory is that errors in *mutuel* odds can be exploited profitably because the prices for the horses most favoured by the betting fraternity, the 'public plays', frequently over-estimate the chance of these short-priced animals relative to less-fancied horses at longer odds. This is borne out by the actual results of races. Form only works out some of the time. Consequently the *mutuel* odds against candidates largely ignored by the public often represent real value. If the so-called overlay on a particular horse is high enough, a bet is justified. Thus odds, not selection criteria, determine what is to be backed. The overlay operator will more often than not be required to support one horse in a race even if, in his personal opinion, another horse is more likely to win.

The overlay concept is not necessarily the one which concentrates exclusively on outsiders however, though that is its tendency. Favourites or near-favourites can be 'under-bet' as well as 'over-bet', and the former would constitute an overlay worthy of exploiting if the price difference compared with the estimated real chance is considered significant enough.

The overlay system may or may not work in the USA. Some extravagant boasts have been made about its successes over the years, though if the idea is really so brilliant, it is not unfair to ask why every American horse-player worth his overlay salt has not long since forsaken the tracks for a life of luxury and ease in some tropical paradise. Be that as it may, in a British context, backing horses for no other reason than that they are thought to be at odds greater than their true form chance seems a suspect proposition.

As we have already noted, British bookmakers make depressingly few mistakes. Any racing enthusiast would surely agree about that. As for Tote prices in this country, they tend to follow, fairly closely, the market established by the bookmakers. True, outsiders on the Tote usually better the bookies' price, but out of the large number of outsiders on every card, how many win?

Betting with the bookmakers or on the Tote, judgements about value have to be made before the start of a race. Just because a horse is at a higher price than it should be, in the backer's estimation, does not mean that it will actually succeed. Even if he can regularly spot what he believes to be significant discrepancies in the odds, the difference still has to be translated into what really matters, namely winners.

If racing is compared to a purely mathematical game like roulette, then a competent player should win against the House in the long run if only he had a mathematical advantage in the odds, just as in reality the casinos make their money from the 'edge' they build into the odds in their own favour. In racing the bookmakers' edge, as explained above, varies between around 10 per cent and 35 per cent on the total number of runners in a race. Can a 'value' system for single selections really offset this degree of disadvantage to the backer?

Realistically, a horse strongly fancied at a price which seems fair is probably the best that serious backers of horses can do, and the right price comes down to personal judgement in the end, not a magic formula. Much more important is to find methods of regularly backing a lot of winners. By contrast, backing strings of horses by price alone, even if the punter has no great faith in their ability to win, is a pill that is not easy to swallow.

This opening chapter sets the tone for the rest of the book. Racing is a hard school and making money from it will always be an uphill struggle. That does not mean that it cannot be done. In racing, as in life, there are ways and means of overcoming most difficulties. So read on.

2
Staking Plans

Graduated Stakes Systems

The aim of all staking plans is to arrange matters so that big stakes go on to winners and small stakes on to losers, the opposite scenario to the examples of bad staking given in Chapter 1. The problem is that the pattern of winners and losers in any sequence can never be known in advance. And, despite the best efforts of all manner of mathematicians and statisticians down the years, no one has ever discovered a way of regulating stakes according to some fixed principle that will accommodate every possible pattern. However, this much is certain mathematically, a staking system on single selections must be based on one or other of two opposite ideas – either it increases after losers or after winners – although it is possible to combine both in one unified method of stakes regulation.

Where there is an increase after losers the hope is that when a winner is found the stakes will have risen sufficiently to wipe out any losses on the sequence so far and to yield a profit overall. There are two problems here. First, when a winner occurs its price in relation to the stake on it might not be good enough to achieve this dual objective. Second, when a losing run is struck, and there will always be losing runs however sound the method of selection, even apparently modest increases have a tendency to produce a high level of staking very rapidly, thereby inevitably straining the backer's nerve and cash resources to the absolute limit. Given infinite quantities of these two latter assets, it is theoretically possible, as we shall see later, for increases always to turn losses into gains, but in practice the random factor in the incidence of winners to losers is extremely difficult to overcome.

On the other hand, when stakes are increased only after winners, many of the above objections no longer apply. Now the backer is not chasing losses but attempting to finance his betting with money from the bookmaker. Profits will mount on a winning run and stakes can be made to drop back quickly to an acceptable level in anticipation of a sequence of losers.

There is however a snag, and a big one at that. Examine the two sequences below on the supposition that there is a one point increase after a winner and an immediate decrease to one point after a loser.

Lost, Won 2–1,Won Evens,Won Evens,Won 3–1,Lost, Lost, Lost

The results of the staking plan are:

| –1 | +2 | +2 | +3 | +12 | –5 | –1 | –1 |

There is an 11-point profit overall, compared with one of only three points at level stakes.

However, if the sequence is rearranged as follows, the staking plan does much less well.

Won 2–1, Lost, Won Evens, Lost, Won Evens Lost, Won 3–1,Lost

Now the outcome is:

| +2 | –2 | +1 | –2 | +1 | –2 | +3 | –2 |

This time there is a loss of one point on a series with exactly the same number of winners and losers.

What all this means is that it is not only the number of winners to losers and the starting prices of winners that matters. Almost as important is the way in which winners fall. Systems like the above calling for increases after winners do best when successful selections occur, for the most part, in consecutive sequence, and the longer such sequences are, the better. Even with short-priced selections likely to give a good percentage of winners however, there is no guarantee that this is a general pattern which will actually occur.

This point is reinforced if increasing after losers is examined in more detail, for here also the backer is gambling on a favourable pattern where the largest stakes will go on winners, not losers.

Let us suppose that stakes are to be increased by one point after each loser and decreased by one point after a winner. This is the result of the first sequence set out above:

Lost, Won 2–1,Won Evens,Won Evens,Won 3–1,Lost, Lost, Lost
 –1   +4   +1   +1   +3   –1   –2   –3

This amounts to a two-point gain against the three points at level stakes.

But look what happens on the second sequence:

Won 2–1, Lost, Won Evens, Lost, Won Evens Lost, Won 3–1,Lost
 +2   –1   +2   –1   +2   –1   +6   –1

This time there is a gain of eight points, a much better result.

However, if the original pattern is rearranged for a second time, the same system of staking produces a complete reversal in the backer's fortunes:

Won 2–1,Won Evens,Won Evens,Won 3–1,Lost, Lost, Lost, Lost
 +2   +1   +1   +3   –1   –2   –3   –4

Now there is no profit at all, but a loss of three points.

Lengthen any of the above sequences to mirror an

actual extended period of betting, and the variations in what any staking plan can achieve will become even more apparent. Everything depends, ultimately, on pattern and the incidence of winners will not always be such as to allow a system of staking to maximise profits or minimise losses. It may do so but, then again, it may not. This is for the simple reason that how winners fall in relation to losers is an unknown at the time betting begins.

All this is emphasised tenfold if extremes of the two types of staking are considered. One is the Reverse Monte Carlo, also known as the Reverse Labouchère system. The other is generally known as 'cover-to-win' or 'retrieve' staking. They are included in this chapter because the author, in his capacity as a reader of racing and betting manuscripts for a well-known publishing house, has seen both plans hailed several times over as 'infallible systems' – the ultimate answer to the problem of beating the bookmaker.

Cover-to-Win System

'Cover-to-win' staking takes the principle of increasing stakes after losers to its absolute limit. In its simplest form the method is to back each selection in a series to win a fixed amount. This will always be the sum of any losses so far plus the intended profit from the coup as a whole. After the first loser the backer adds his loss on to the original target-profit figure and then increases his stake on the next bet according to the odds available, in order to achieve the new target figure should the horse win. Betting continues in this manner until a winner occurs, thereby winning back the accumulated deficit as well as producing the desired profit on the coup.

According to its protagonists the system works because it is the only way of achieving the seemingly impossible. It does actually succeed in guaranteeing that the largest stake in a series must fall on a winner, and in such a way that inevitably a profit is bound to accrue.

This all sounds deceptively easy and the most deceptive thing about it is that for a lot of the time it succeeds, provided bets are confined to the type of selection which can be expected to yield a good percentage of winners without worrying too much about starting prices. But take for example the following series of bets where five losers and a single winner at short odds represents a very low level of success in punting terms. Like all the examples in Chapter 2, the stakes are shown pre-tax for simplicity's sake and are exact to the nearest 1p so that the method can be followed in detail. In practice, when actually placing bets with a bookmaker, odd amounts would have to be rounded up or down to the nearest 5p or 10p and tax paid on stakes or winnings.

COVER-TO-WIN SYSTEM – EXAMPLE 1

Target	Price	Stake	Result	Profit	Loss	Accumulated Profit (+) or Loss (−)
£10.00	3–1	£3.33	Lost		£3.33	−£3.33
£13.33	7–2	£3.81	Lost		£3.81	−£7.14
£17.14	6–1	£2.86	Lost		£2.86	−£10.00
£20.00	3–1	£6.67	Lost		£6.67	−£16.67
£26.67	2–1	£13.34	Lost		£13.34	−£30.01
£40.01	11–8	£29.10	Won	£40.01		+£10.00

Everything is fine. Despite a hefty loss at level stakes on the sequence, the cover-to-win formula has actually achieved its objective of a £10 gain, and this without too much betting capital being placed at risk.

However, if the next example is studied closely, it becomes apparent that terrific problems can occur on a less favourable series of bets:

COVER-TO-WIN SYSTEM – EXAMPLE 2

Target	Price	Stake	Result	Profit	Loss	Accumulated Profit (+) or Loss (–)
£10.00	13–8	£6.15	Lost		£6.15	–£6.15
£16.15	7–4	£9.23	Lost		£9.23	–£15.38
£25.38	4–5	£31.73	Lost		£31.73	–£47.11
£57.11	3–1	£19.04	Lost		£19.04	–£66.15
£76.15	Evens	£76.15	Lost		£76.15	–£142.30
£152.30	3–1	£50.77	Lost		£50.77	–£193.07
£203.07	2–1	£101.54	Lost		£101.54	–£294.61
£304.61	4–6	£456.92	Lost		£456.92	–£751.53
£761.53	4–5	£951.91	Won	£761.53		+£10.00

True, the backer has made his £10, but at what risk? On a sequence of only nine bets he has been forced to stake a total of £1703.44 to win what, by comparison, is the trivial amount of £10. Cover-to-win staking embroiled him in a capital outlay completely out of proportion to the expected gain.

There are two reasons for this. First, the losing run has extended beyond just a handful of bets and second, every time a horse at odds on is to be backed, the stake jumps to a dizzy height. 'Very well' says the cover-to-win enthusiast, 'the problem is quite easily solved – there is no bet if the selection starts at odds-on'. But the trouble with this is that as soon as the runners at the shortest prices are eliminated, the ratio of winners to losers could easily decrease, and the plan's other bugbear, an extended losing run, may decisively come into play, once again causing the stakes to spiral dangerously out of proportion.

Anyone inclined to reject these arguments on the grounds that they are based on an imaginary illustration should dip into the Form Book. Cover-to-win staking is almost always operated on favourites, but there are plenty of examples in the record of results where favourites run up long losing sequences. Take for example a recent big

August meeting at York. Here is the record of favourites over the three days, with the necessary stakes for cover-to-win £10 on each completed coup at the meeting.

COVER-TO-WIN SYSTEM – REALITY

Race No. Horse	Target	Price	Stake	Result	Profit	Loss	Accumulated Profit (+) or Loss (–)
Day One							
1 In Command	£10.00	8–11	£13.75	Lost		£13.75	–£13.75
2 Berlin Blue Private Song	£23.75	7–2	£6.79	Lost		£6.79	–£20.54
3 Halling	£30.54	6–4	£20.36	Won	£30.54		+£10.00
4 Royal Court	£10.00	11–4	£3.64	Lost		£3.64	–£3.64
5 Double Splendour	£13.64	4–1	£3.41	Lost		£3.41	–£7.05
6 Celeric	£17.05	9–4	£7.58	Won	£17.06		+£10.01
7 Demolition Man	£10.00	11–4	£3.64	Lost		£3.64	–£3.64
Day Two							
1 Swiss Coast	£13.64	3–1	£4.55	Lost		£4.55	–£8.19
2 Shamadara	£18.19	2–1	£9.10	Lost		£9.10	–£17.29
3 Harbour Dues Corradini	£27.29	7–1	£3.90	Lost		£3.90	–£21.19
4 The West	£31.19	2–1	£15.60	Lost		£15.60	–£36.79
5 Fahim	£46.79	7–4	£26.74	Lost		£26.74	–£63.53
6 Tipsy Creek	£73.53	6–4	£49.02	Lost		£49.02	–£112.55
7 Clan Chief Zalotti	£122.55	11–2	£22.28	Lost		£22.28	–£134.83
Day Three							
1 Elnadim	£144.83	11–8	£105.33	Lost		£105.33	–£240.16
2 Seeba	£250.16	11–4	£90.97	Lost		£90.97	–£331.13
3 Mind Games	£341.13	7–4	£194.93	Lost		£194.93	–£526.06
4 Intidab North Song	£536.06	11–2	£97.47	Lost		£97.47	–£623.53
5 Dacha	£633.53	11–2	£115.19	Lost		£115.19	–£738.72
6 Annaba	£748.72	3–1	£249.57	Lost		£249.57	–£988.29
7 Ali-Royal	£998.29	100–30	£299.49	Lost		£299.49	–£1287.78

This is a classic case of stakes getting completely out of control in a plan that increases after losers. The cover-to-win operator has won £10 twice, but lost £1287.78 in just three days at this York meeting. Even choosing correctly between the several joint favourites would not have helped, since they all lost.

However attractive in theory, cover-to-win staking is a fool's paradise. Most of the time it does win. Provided it is worked on selections which give a good percentage of winners overall, it goes merrily on its way producing small, but steady gains. The punter, lured into a false sense of security, shouts 'Eureka!' and thinks that at last he has found the answer to his problem. A steady income from racing is there for the taking. But sooner or later the crash always comes. One disastrous losing run will destroy all the accumulated profits, stakes escalate to ridiculously high levels and the punter without unlimited financial means for betting is suddenly face-to-face with ruin.

The Reverse Labouchère System

Another staking plan often credited with near-magical properties is the Reverse Labouchère system borrowed from the world of the casino. In that context it has sometimes been operated with great success by syndicates working the even chances at roulette. As with all staking systems a favourable pattern of results is essential if it is to deliver the goods. So, while most members of a roulette team playing the system will sit for hours winning a little or losing a little on balance, very occasionally one of them will strike a sequence that enables Reverse Labouchère to run up a huge profit very quickly. Needless to say, such syndicates are heavily discouraged by casino managements.

When used for betting on horses it must be worked only on favourites offering the prospect of a high winning percentage, and the fact that a horse is likely to start at odds-on is no reason for excluding it. The system is one which calls for increases in stakes after winners. As we have seen, a large gain will only accrue from such systems if strings of consecutive, or near consecutive, winners feature regularly in the pattern of results. Winners rather than prices are the most important consideration.

The system's rules can be summarised thus:

1 Write down a series of consecutive numbers from 1 upwards. For horse racing 1 2 3 4 5 6 7 is recommended. This 'line' will be the initial arbiter of stakes and is adjusted after each bet.

2 Always stake the sum of the first and last number in the line. Cross these off after a loser, but add the winning stake to the end of the line after a winner.

3 If all the numbers in a line are eventually crossed off, start a new line of 1 to 7.

The effect of these rules is that stakes rise very sharply on a run of winners, but are cut back fairly gradually when losers are encountered. A high level of staking throughout is a characteristic of the plan.

The author has seen some very extravagant claims made for this plan over the years, and there is no doubt that a very handsome gain can be amassed very quickly on those occasions when the backer can do no wrong when it comes to selecting winners.

However, as a fair initial test for the plan, the sequence below has been constructed. From the 36 selections there are 15 winners and a level stakes profit of 12.83 points. Despite the sound winning percentage, winners and losers tend to alternate fairly regularly. There are no long winning runs which we know in advance will help the plan to succeed.

Line	Stake	Result	Accumulated Profit (+) or Loss (−)
1 2 3 4 5 6 7	£8.00	Lost	−£8.00
~~1~~ 2 3 4 5 6 ~~7~~	£8.00	Lost	−£16.00
~~2~~ 3 4 5 ~~6~~	£8.00	Won 5–2	+£4.00
3 4 5 8	£11.00	Won 4–6	+£11.37
3 4 5 8 11	£14.00	Lost	−£2.63
~~3~~ 4 5 8 ~~11~~	£12.00	Lost	−£14.63
4 5 ~~8~~	£5.00	Lost	−£19.63
~~5~~ – 1 2 3 4 5 6 7	£8.00	Won 7–2	+£8.37
1 2 3 4 5 6 7 8	£9.00	Lost	−£0.63
~~1~~ 2 3 4 5 6 7 ~~8~~	£9.00	Lost	−£9.63
~~2~~ 3 4 5 6 ~~7~~	£9.00	Lost	−£18.63
~~3~~ 4 5 ~~6~~	£9.00	Won 11–8	−£6.21
4 5 9	£13.00	Won 9–4	+£23.04
4 5 9 13	£17.00	Won 3–1	+£74.04
4 5 9 13 17	£21.00	Lost	+£53.04
4 5 9 13 ~~17~~	£18.00	Lost	+£35.04
~~5~~ 9 ~~13~~	£9.00	Won 5–2	+£57.54
9 9	£18.00	Lost	+£39.54
~~9~~ ~~9~~ – 1 2 3 4 5 6 7	£8.00	Won 5–4	+£49.54
1 2 3 4 5 6 7 8	£9.00	Won 4–1	+£85.54
1 2 3 4 5 6 7 8 9	£10.00	Lost	+£75.54
~~1~~ 2 3 4 5 6 7 8 ~~9~~	£10.00	Lost	+£65.54
~~2~~ 3 4 5 6 7 ~~8~~	£10.00	Won 4–5	+£73.54
3 4 5 6 7 10	£13.00	Lost	+£60.54
~~3~~ 4 5 6 7 ~~10~~	£11.00	Lost	+£49.54
4 5 6 ~~7~~	£11.00	Lost	+£38.54
~~5~~ ~~6~~ – 1 2 3 4 5 6 7	£8.00	Won 9–4	+£56.54
1 2 3 4 5 6 7 8	£9.00	Lost	+£47.54
~~1~~ 2 3 4 5 6 7 ~~8~~	£9.00	Won 13–8	+£62.21
2 3 4 5 6 7 9	£11.00	Lost	+£51.21
~~2~~ 3 4 5 6 7 ~~9~~	£10.00	Lost	+£41.21
~~3~~ 4 5 6 ~~7~~	£10.00	Won 5–1	+£91.21
4 5 6 10	£14.00	Won 11–10	+£106.61
4 5 6 10 14	£18.00	Won 2–1	+£142.61
4 5 6 10 14 18	£22.00	Lost	+£120.61
4 5 6 10 14 ~~18~~	£19.00	Lost	+£101.61

At first glance a final gain of £101.61 looks a very fair outcome and seems to vindicate the system, even though there are no long winning runs which would have certainly spiralled stakes and profits in the space of only a few bets. On the other hand the opening stake is one of £8, and if this is counted as one point, in level stakes terms £8 × 12.83 points profit = £102.64 is much the same result.

On the next sequence however the real strengths, and also the weaknesses of Reverse Labouchere are much more evident.

REVERSE LABOUCHÈRE SYSTEM – EXAMPLE 2

Line	Stake	Result	Accumulated Profit (+) or Loss (−)
1 2 3 4 5 6 7	£8.00	Won 2–1	+£16.00
1 2 3 4 5 6 7 8	£9.00	Won 3–1	+£43.00
1 2 3 4 5 6 7 8 9	£10.00	Won 4–6	+£49.70
1 2 3 4 5 6 7 8 9 10	£11.00	Lost	+£38.70
1 2 3 4 5 6 7 8 9 10	£11.00	Lost	+£27.70
2 3 4 5 6 7 8 9	£11.00	Lost	+£16.70
3 4 5 6 7 8	£11.00	Won 6–4	+£33.20
4 5 6 7 11	£15.00	Won 2–1	+£63.20
4 5 6 7 11 15	£19.00	Won 11–10	+£84.10
4 5 6 7 11 15 19	£23.00	Lost	+£61.10
4 5 6 7 11 15 19	£20.00	Won 1–2	+£71.10
5 6 7 11 15 20	£25.00	Won 4–7	+£85.35
5 6 7 11 15 20 25	£30.00	Won 4–6	+£105.45
5 6 7 11 15 20 25 30	£35.00	Won 6–4	+£157.95
5 6 7 11 15 20 25 30 35	£40.00	Won 11–8	+£213.15
5 6 7 11 15 20 25 30 35 40	£45.00	Lost	+£168.15
5 6 7 11 15 20 25 30 35 40	£41.00	Lost	+£127.15
6 7 11 15 20 25 30 35	£37.00	Lost	+£90.15
7 11 15 20 25 30	£36.00	Lost	+£54.15
11 15 20 25	£35.00	Lost	+£19.15
15 20 – 1 2 3 4 5 6 7	£8.00	Won 2–1	+£35.15

This sequence, although a relatively short one, tells us all that we need to know about the Reverse Labouchère system. Runs of three, three and five consecutive winners enable the plan to improve considerably on level stakes and it shows a marvellous gain of £213.15 after only 15 bets. But the fall from the heights is devastatingly sudden and swift. In the space of only five more bets profits have dwindled to a mere £19.15!

Reverse Labouchère staking, therefore, must be operated with a pre-determined 'check-out' point. On an opening stake of £8, a gain of £100 seems a reasonable goal. This should be set aside as an accumulated gain and the stake put back immediately to the original £8 as the starting point of a fresh coup, again with a target of £100. Anyone who cannot resist the temptation to go on betting past a reasonable check-out invariably runs a grave risk of seeing everything that has been gained dissipated in double-quick time.

With a £100 check-out on the above sequence this would have been the excellent result:

REVERSE LABOUCHÈRE SYSTEM – EXAMPLE 3 WITH A CHECK-OUT

Line	Stake	Result	Accumulated Profit (+) or Loss (−)
5 6 7 11 15 20 25	£30.00	Won 4–6	+£105.45
1 2 3 4 5 6 7	£8.00	Won 6–4	+£12.00
1 2 3 4 5 6 7 8	£9.00	Won 11–8	+£24.42
1 2 3 4 5 6 7 8 9	£10.00	Lost	+£14.42
~~1~~ 2 3 4 5 6 7 8 ~~9~~	£10.00	Lost	+£4.42
~~2~~ 3 4 5 6 7 ~~8~~	£10.00	Lost	−£5.58
~~3~~ 4 5 6 ~~7~~	£10.00	Lost	−£15.58
4 5 ~~6~~	£5.00	Lost	−£20.58
~~5~~ – 1 2 3 4 5 6 7	£8.00	Won 2–1	−£4.58

Provided the check-out procedure is strictly observed, the author has no hesitation in saying that, on the right kind of selection, Reverse Labouchère is the best staking system he has ever encountered. Barring freak patterns of results, it is unlikely to worsen the level-stakes position by much and on a favourable pattern can do much to improve it. It cannot be stressed enough, however, that the operator needs both a cool nerve and a highly disciplined attitude to betting if he is to get the best from the plan. One or two bets too many at the height of a successful run may be fatal, and any tendency to greed can be punished severely. It is also the height of folly to attempt to work the plan on anything but short-priced selections.

Level Stakes and Other Alternatives

It is fair to say that the backer can never go far wrong with level stakes, whilst staking plans carry varying degrees of risk in addition to the normal factors of chance involved in selecting horses and betting on them.

One alternative to staking plans calling for the rigid regulation of stakes is to increase stakes generally for a period, if and when a worthwhile profit has accrued in the medium term. This calls for very sound judgement on the part of the backer, but may be the best hope of speeding up the process by which a worthwhile sum can be amassed with an equal amount bet on every horse. If profits continue to grow, the general level of staking can then be increased again when the time seems appropriate. Equally, should things go badly, a general adjustment in the opposite direction may tide the punter over a bad patch.

The racing enthusiast has choices in staking as in other areas of betting. Many will stand by level stakes, and there is an old maxim in racing that if a system cannot succeed at level stakes, then it cannot succeed at all. This is not strictly true. A staking plan can enhance profits but equally, the same plan may do worse than level stakes on a different and less favourable rota of results. Even a really sound staking method, for example Reverse Labouchère, can have its failures. This could be because of insufficient winners, the wrong pattern of results, or because the operator misjudges the situation and ends up losing all or most of what has been gained.

If level stakes are preferred in principle to formulae which vary the stakes from bet to bet, it is still possible to adjust the general level of staking in response to results. As an open-ended solution to the staking problem this has a lot of appeal but even here it is easy to make a mistake, for without foreknowledge the right time for a general increase or reduction in stakes will always be difficult to judge. When to take a good profit out of the betting continuum altogether and drop stakes back to something like their opening level is another imponderable that the backer is just as likely to get wrong as right. It will always be safer to cash in a big gain and start again, but in doing so greater profits still may be missed from playing up winnings should results continue to favour the punter.

There are, however, other options which, even if they are usually a great deal more hazardous, also offer the chance of much greater rewards in relation to outlay. These options are considered in detail in the next two chapters.

Conclusions

Staking has always been a contentious subject among those who bet on horses, but after the survey in this chapter it is possible to arrive at a set of conclusions which ought to settle matters, if not once and for all then at least in such a way that a lot of good wood is separated from the controversial trees.

    1 Unless the backer's capital is unlimited and a bookmaker can be found to accept bets to any

amount, no staking plan can guarantee a profit before betting commences.

2 With the exception of the very risky, cover-to-win method which calls for unlimited resources, no staking plan can be constructed which will turn a big loss into a big profit.

3 Most staking plans will, at best, improve only marginally on level stakes.

4 Any staking plan can worsen the level stakes position in the event of an unfavourable results pattern.

5 Plans which increase after losers may well not achieve their objective, and those calling for sharp increases in stakes can get the backer into deep water very quickly. Whatever the rate of increase, all plans of this kind involve chasing losses.

6 Increasing stakes after winners is recommended. Plans that increase the stakes gradually can do the backer little harm and may do some good. They are, it must be remembered, as much dependent on 'pattern' as any other sort of plan. When profits are boosted dramatically, careful managing is required if the backer is to emerge in a good position in the long term. Here the system operator can be likened to a financial investment manager who must decide when to take profits on the stocks and shares in which he deals.

7 Anyone using a staking plan of any type should avoid outsiders and even medium-priced selections which may produce long runs of losers.

3

Racing Permutations

Introduction

Properly adjusted staking on single selections is the safest way to restrict losses and enhance profits, but for the ordinary punter the relatively limited betting bank he has at his disposal means that any overall gain achieved will be correspondingly modest. An alternative to large stakes on singles is clever staking on cumulative wagers, based on doubles, trebles and accumulators, with which big wins are possible for only a small outlay. This approach obviously carries a greater element of risk, but speculative wagers of this sort can be constructed in such a way that steady profits may accrue even if a huge pay out from a single coup eludes the backer. The use of racing perms, therefore, could in practice turn out to have a double vindication.

Popular Permutations

It is probably true to say that most racing enthusiasts have only a vague understanding of the complicated subject of permutation. Though perms are standard fare in Pools betting for instance, they are much less common in horse racing. In fact the limit of most punter's forays into the field is the following series of popular bets:

Number of selections	Outlay in points	Name	Singles	Doubles	Trebles	Four-folds	Five-folds	Six-folds	Seven-folds
3	7	PATENT	3	3	1	—	—	—	—
4	11	YANKEE	—	6	4	1	—	—	—
5	26	CANADIAN or SUPER YANKEE	—	10	10	5	1	—	—
6	57	HEINZ	—	15	20	15	6	1	—
7	120	MULTI	—	21	35	35	21	7	1

The problem with these wagers, certainly the more ambitious of them, is that they only really pay off when all, or nearly all, of the punter's selections go in. Any reasonable win expectancy on the other hand results in a large wastage in stakes. For example, here is the position with the HEINZ bet when three winners are included:

WINNING BETS:
Doubles   3
Trebles   1

LOSING BETS:
Doubles   12
Trebles   19
Fourfolds   15
Fivefolds   6
Sixfold   1

Evidently prices would have to be very good indeed for the punter even to recover his outlay, let alone start winning, on this rota of bets.

Reduction Plans – Doubles

With well-designed racing permutations, however, it is possible to go a long way towards cutting down on the damaging wastage of stakes.

Consider this simplest of examples:

Selections: A B C D
Two doubles: AC and BD

Thus, there are just two bets as against the usual six doubles on the four selections, yet there is a guarantee that three winners must produce a winning double. If either A or C are both successful, or B and D, the bet can win with less than the number of winners stipulated by the guarantee.

This type of arrangement is known as a reduction plan, and it can easily be extended to a greater number of selections by the simple rule of dividing the horses selected into two equal, or as equal as possible, groups and then backing each group with the number of doubles needed for full cover.

Here are plans for five, six and seven selections:

<blockquote>
A
B   3 doubles
<u>C</u>
D   1 double
E
</blockquote>

Total: 4 doubles

Guarantee: one winning double if three winners are included among the five selections; three winning doubles if all in one section.

<blockquote>
A
B   3 doubles
<u>C</u>
D
E   3 doubles
F
</blockquote>

Total: 6 doubles

Guarantee: at least one winning double if three winners are included in the six selections; three winning doubles if all in one section.

$$
\left.\begin{array}{l} A \\ B \\ C \\ D \end{array}\right\} \quad \text{6 doubles}
$$

$$
\left.\begin{array}{l} E \\ F \\ G \end{array}\right\} \quad \text{3 doubles}
$$

Total: 9 doubles

Guarantee: at least one winning double if three winners are included in the seven selections; three winning doubles if all in one section.

In these examples prices need not be exceptional to recover outlay, provided the guarantee is met. In the last bet three winners priced at no worse than 2–1 would automatically win back the total stake, except for the betting tax. Just two winners at that price would do the same should they fall together in either the top or bottom section of the wager, and better prices in either eventuality would naturally produce a profit, as would any number of winners over and above the minimum depending on how they are distributed among the nine possible doubles.

Reduction Plans – Trebles

It is easy enough to extend this idea to trebles, using the same basic formula of dividing the total number of selections into three groups as equal as possible, before covering for trebles from group to group in rotation:

$$
\left.\begin{array}{l} A \\ B \end{array}\right\} \quad \text{Perm A and B with C or D}
$$
= 1 × 2 = 2 trebles

$$
\left.\begin{array}{l} C \\ D \end{array}\right\} \quad \text{Perm C and D with E or F}
$$
= 1 × 2 = 2 trebles

$$
\left.\begin{array}{l} E \\ F \end{array}\right\} \quad \text{Perm E and F with A or B}
$$
= 1 × 2 = 2 trebles

Total: 6 trebles

Guarantee: at least one winning treble, possibly more, if four winners are included in the six selections.

Also, regardless of the guarantee, the punter would be justified in feeling slightly aggrieved if he backed three winners and the perm failed to line up a winning treble, although obviously this could happen.

To make sure that readers fully understand the principle involved with these bets, this is the formula for trebles stated in full:

1 Combine the number of possible doubles in the first group with each single selection in the second group.
2 Combine all the doubles in the second group with each selection in the third group.
3 Take the possible doubles in the third group with each selection in the first group.
4 If any group has three or more selections stake on the actual number of trebles within it, in addition to the doubles.

These two examples illustrate the operation of the complete formula:

A	Perm two of A B and C with D or E
B	= 3 × 2 = 6 trebles
C	Perm D and E with F or G
D	= 1 × 2 = 2 trebles
E	Perm F and G with A B or C
F	= 1 × 3 = 3 trebles
G	Perm A B and C = 1 treble

Total: 12 trebles

Guarantee: at least one winning treble; possibly more if four winners are included in the seven selections.

And again:

A	Perm two of A B C and D with E F or G
B	= 6 × 3 = 18 trebles
C	Perm two of E F and G with H I or J
D	= 3 × 3 = 9 trebles
E	Perm two of H I and J with A B C or D
F	= 3 × 4 = 12 trebles
G	Perm three of A B C and D = 4 trebles
H	Perm E F and G = 1 treble
I	Perm H I and J = 1 treble
J	

Total: 45 trebles

Guarantee: at least one winning treble; possibly more if four winners are included in the ten selections.

When submitting bets of this sort to a bookmaker, they should be written out in the way shown below, giving the name of the selection first, followed by the letter, and adding on the appropriate instructions. Here is one for eight selections with the usual guarantee of a treble from four winners, and possibly only three.

THE BUTLER	A	Perm two of A B and C with D E or F
DEVON VICTORY	B	= 3 × 3 = 9 trebles
VENATE	C	Perm two of D E and F with G or H
OBERON	D	= 3 × 2 = 6 trebles
NO CATCH	E	Perm G and H with A B or C
ROSE OF DAMASCUS	F	= 1 × 3 = 3 trebles
DIAMOND GIRL	G	Perm A B and C = 1 treble
OFFICE BOY	H	Perm D E and F = 1 treble
		Total: 20 trebles

Recalling the earlier doubles formula, the same selections can be backed with a guarantee of one winning double from three successful nominations:

THE BUTLER	
DEVON VICTORY	6 doubles
VENATE	
OBERON	
NO CATCH	
ROSE OF DAMASCUS	6 doubles
DIAMOND GIRL	
OFFICE BOY	

Total: 12 doubles

Compound Perms and Accumulators

It is also possible to devise compound wagers which include accumulators as well as doubles and trebles. Here the aim is obviously a huge pay out, with the doubles providing an element of insurance against things not going exactly according to plan. A series of such bets is set out below. They range from wagers with only limited aspirations right up to the most ambitious assault on the bookmaker, but all give an excellent balance between cost and cover, and all have unshakeable guarantees. They are, therefore, much more than just hopeful gambles.

Five horses: A B C D E – 12 bets.
4 doubles: AD AE BC DE
3 trebles: ABD ABE CDE
5 fourfolds: ABCD ABCE ABDE ACDE BCDE

Minimum guarantees: three winners must give a double; four winners give two doubles, one treble and one fourfold.

Six horses: A B C D E F – 12 bets.
6 doubles: AC AF BD BE CF DE
6 trebles: ABE ACE ADF BCD BCF DEF

Minimum guarantees: three winners must give a double. Four winners must give one double and one treble.

Six horses: A B C D E F – 10 bets.
5 doubles: AB BC CD DE EF
4 trebles: ACE ACF ADE BDF
1 fourfold: ABEF

Minimum guarantees: Three winners must give either a double or a treble. Four winners give either three doubles, or two doubles and one treble, or two trebles, or two doubles. Five winners give four doubles and one treble, or three doubles, two trebles and one fourfold, or three doubles and three trebles.

Six horses: A B C D E F – 17 bets
6 doubles: AC AF BD BE CF DE
8 trebles: ACE ACF ADE ADF BCE BCF BDE BDF
3 fourfolds: ABCD ABEF CDEF

Minimum guarantees: Three winners must give a double. A winner in each of pairs A and B, C and D, E and F gives a treble. If two of these pairs all contain winners, there will be a fourfold.

Less patient backers may baulk at having to write out in full each component in the above wagers, but here is a plan which can be entered with little effort on just a few betting slips. It guarantees a massive pay out for an all-correct entry, with outstanding returns in the event of a near miss.

Seven horses: A B C D E F G – 77 bets.
7 Yankees (6 doubles, 4 trebles and a fourfold):
ABCF ABDE ACEG ADFG BCDG BEFG CDEF

Minimum guarantee: Five winners give the all-important fourfold which must produce a successful Yankee. Six winners give the cast-iron certainty of three winning Yankees. In both cases there will be outside doubles and trebles in support. Even with four winners a Yankee is still possible and this number of correct forecasts, or even three or just two, will always give the punter some kind of consolation prize, the size of which will depend upon the prices and pattern of winners.

The principle of accumulated odds networking the same winners across the seven component Yankees makes this a real blockbuster of a bet, ideally suited to building up impressive gains, in particular from short-priced selections, where a high win-frequency is to be expected.

Another bet, less ambitious but equally effective in its way, again where the punter does not have to write out the names of his selections many times over, is set out below. Note that the horses must be numbered 1 to 6.

1	ROYAL DESIRE	Perm five consecutive doubles,
2	GRAND TOUR	four non-consecutive trebles, and
3	FAIR SHOW	numbers 1 2 3 4, numbers 1 2 5 6
4	LIMEVILLE	and numbers 3 4 5 6 in fourfolds
5	MACEDONIA	
6	RED PEAK	Total: 12 bets

A full check of all the wagers involved is as follows:

	Doubles			Trebles			Fourfolds	
1	X			X	X	X	X	X
2	X	X				X	X	X
3		X	X	X	X		X	X
4		X	X		X	X	X	X
5			X	X	X		X	X
6			X		X	X	X	X

This is a rather subtle arrangement in which three winners must yield a double and five winners a fourfold. Four correct guarantees either one double and one treble, or at the very worst a minimum of two doubles.

Finally, for those who prefer quantity rather than quality in their betting and like an interest in a large number of races, the pairs approach, though very risky, has the potential to win big if it clicks. The idea is to select a large number of horses in different races and to back them for fourfolds in the following manner:

12 selections

DOMESDAY ⎫
OUR CHARGER ⎭

DOMACILE ⎫
RELICARIO ⎭

SKATE IN ⎫   Perm any two bracketed pairs
TONIN ⎭   of selections from six pairs

BEOTIEN ⎫   for fourfolds = 15 fourfolds
LEGAL ART ⎭

WILD ROSE ⎫
BLUE MURDER ⎭

GRECIAN FLAG ⎫
ON APPROVAL ⎭

Here is a table which shows how many fourfolds are involved when a greater number of selections right up to 24 are covered in this way:

Selections	Pairs	Fourfolds
14	7	21
16	8	28
18	9	36
20	10	45
22	11	55
24	12	66

Winners *have* to fall together in pairs to count, and for this reason these are not the most professional of wagers, but they might appeal to someone who bets in very small amounts mostly for interest, but with the ever-present hope of a big win in the back of his mind. They are included here in what is a scientific treatise on racing as 'fun' bets, but they are offered without apology and in the knowledge that tastes vary in betting as much as in any other area of life.

Whatever readers take away from this chapter on permutation, it must now be clear that there is much more to betting than the tired old wagers pushed routinely over betting-shop counters by most punters every day. Racing perms take a wide range, and unlike most of the fancy bets promoted so aggressively by the bookmaking fraternity in their marketing and advertising, the best of them have very sound credentials as profit makers.

4

Combination Bets

Introduction

Most backers, contemplating bets on doubles, trebles and accumulators, think in terms of only one selection per race. However, with the aid of some straightforward combination mathematics, it is perfectly feasible to enhance the probability of all-correct forecasts by covering two or more runners in opposition, in each of a series of events. Since, dead-heats apart, only one horse can win a race, this will always involve wasted stakes on losing animals. However, the principle governing cumulative bets whereby the odds of winners, plus one point, are multiplied together to arrive at the total return from a successful wager, means that the backer can be rewarded with a profit despite the inevitable loss of a part of his outlay.

Doubles

Take as an example the following bet which may easily produce acceptable gains on carefully selected non-handicaps where first and second favourites tend to monopolise results:

Race 1
Race 2   24 doubles on
Race 3   first and second
Race 4   favourites

£24 plus £2.16 tax paid = £26.16 staked

Provided races in which the first favourite is likely to start at odds on are avoided, a good win is always on the cards from such a bet. Here is the full return from four winners at fairly short prices:

Race 1:   Second Favourite Won 11–4
Race 2:   Favourite Won 7–4
Race 3:   Favourite Won 2–1
Race 4:   Second Favourite Won 100–30

Double Races 1 and 2
Return: £1 × 3.75 × 2.75 = £10.31
Double Races 1 and 3
Return: £1 × 3.75 × 3.00 = £11.25
Double Races 1 and 4
Return: £1 × 3.75 × 4.33 = £16.24
Double Races 2 and 3
Return: £1 × 2.75 × 3.00 = £8.25
Double Races 2 and 4
Return: £1 × 2.75 × 4.33 = £11.91
Double Races 3 and 4
Return: £1 × 3.00 × 4.33 = £12.99

TOTAL RETURN:	£70.95
OUTLAY:	£26.16
NET PROFIT:	£44.79

Thus, despite the luxury of backing two horses in each of four races, the bet has done very well indeed, measured by its return on outlay. Even three winners from eight nominations would always yield some sort of profit on any three of the prices shown, and just two would recover at least part of the total amount originally staked on the whole bet.

Combination bets of this type can be used on named horses as well as favourites. The backer's problem, apart from the very obvious and important one of locating sound selections for a wager, is to calculate the number of bets involved each time, assuming he wishes to vary the number of horses in a race according to how he assesses chances.

In the first place, however, it will help the reader's understanding if the 24 doubles in the above illustration are written out in full:

Favourite (Race 1) with Favourite (Race 2)
Favourite (Race 1) with Favourite (Race 3)
Favourite (Race 1) with Favourite (Race 4)
Favourite (Race 1) with Second favourite (Race 2)
Favourite (Race 1) with Second favourite (Race 3)
Favourite (Race 1) with Second favourite (Race 4)
Second favourite (Race 1) with Favourite (Race 2)
Second favourite (Race 1) with Favourite (Race 3)
Second favourite (Race 1) with Favourite (Race 4)
Second favourite (Race 1) with Second favourite (Race 2)
Second favourite (Race 1) with Second favourite (Race 3)
Second favourite (Race 1) with Second favourite (Race 4)
Favourite (Race 2) with Favourite (Race 3)
Favourite (Race 2) with Favourite (Race 4)
Favourite (Race 2) with Second favourite (Race 3)
Favourite (Race 2) with Second favourite (Race 4)
Second favourite (Race 2) with Favourite (Race 3)
Second favourite (Race 2) with Favourite (Race 4)
Second favourite (Race 2) with Second favourite (Race 3)
Second favourite (Race 2) with Second favourite (Race 4)
Favourite (Race 3) with Favourite (Race 4)
Favourite (Race 3) with Second favourite (Race 4)
Second favourite (Race 3) with Favourite (Race 4)
Second favourite (Race 3) with Second favourite (Race 4)

In fact such long hand is unnecessary in practice. There is a simple formula which will calculate how many doubles are required for different numbers of horses in varying numbers of races. This is it:

Count the total number of selections. Multiply this number by one less than the total and divide by two. From the result deduct the aggregate of the possible two-selection combinations in each separate race.

Therefore in the doubles bet on the first and second favourites in four races, there were a total of eight selections. Multiply this by one less than eight to give $8 \times 7 = 56$, and divide by two $= 28$. In each of the four races there is one combination of two selections, that is the favourite with the second favourite, which cannot win. Deducting these four from 28 gives the correct total of 24 doubles needed to back the two betting-market leaders in the four chosen races.

Here is another example, this time for named selections and involving differing numbers of horses in only three legs:

Race 1:   SILVER DAY
            WELSH MOUNTAIN
            NETHERBY
Race 2:   SECURITY RISK
Race 3:   SELLY OAK
            SKI CHAMPION

Now there is a total of six selections. The formula provided gives the following number of doubles:

$$\frac{6 \times 5}{2} = 15$$

In Race 1 the three horses can be linked so as to give three combinations of two (Silver Day with Welsh Mountain, Silver Day with Netherby, Welsh Mountain with Netherby). Since only one horse is selected for Race 2, no combinations are possible there. In Race 3 Selly Oak and Ski Champion can be combined once. There are thus four combinations to be deducted from 15, producing a total of 11 doubles to be staked on.

The bet's instructions would be written as follows:

Cover for 11 £1 doubles
= £11 plus 99p tax paid
= £11.99 staked

When the winners of all three races are found, there will be three successful doubles, whilst two winners give one winning double. As always with combination bets, very short-priced selections must be avoided if a less than all-correct forecast is to show a profit or at least to recover a worthwhile part of the outlay.

If the above wager had had four selections in the first leg, rather than three, the total number of selections would become seven, giving

$$\frac{7 \times 6}{2} = 21$$

From this would be subtracted any two from four, that is six combinations in Race 1, none in Race 2 as before, and one in Race 3 again – seven ineffective combinations – yielding 14 doubles in all.

Trebles

Turning now to trebles, backing more than one horse in some or all of just three races presents few problems. All that is necessary to determine how many trebles must be staked on, is to multiply together the number of selections in each event. For example:

Race 1:   CALL BOX
           SABLE SKIN
           KING'S DOWN

Race 2:   LADY JULIE

Race 3:   ALESSANDRO
           ANOTHER RONDO
           CANDY FLAKE

           One selection in each race
           = 3 × 1 × 3 = 9 £1 trebles
           = £9 plus 81p tax paid
           = £9.81 staked

If King's Down at 4–1, Lady Julie at 6–4 and Candy Flake at 11–2 are the winners of the three races, the return will be 5 × 2.5 × 6.5 = 81.25, or £81.25 to a £1 stake, yielding a net profit of £71.44 on the £9.81 outlay.

When the strategy is applied to more than three races, however, the procedure to establish the total number of bets is slightly more complicated.

Take this rota of bets:

Race 1:   AFRICAN SLIPPER
           GRAND PRINCE

Race 2:   CAT'S WHISKER

Race 3:   CROUPIER
           BLUE LAGOON

Race 4:   COUNTRY CLUB
           CHYRIA
           SHAHID
           THE SQUIRE

The starting point for calculations is always to write out in full which trebles will be successful should one of the selections in each leg manage to win. Four races involve four trebles, five races 10 trebles, six races 20 trebles and seven races 35 trebles. In this case four races could produce these four winning trebles:

Races 1 2 and 3
Races 1 2 and 4
Races 1 3 and 4
Races 2 3 and 4

Now it is a simple matter to treat each combination of races as a separate entity, and to multiply the number of selections within it to arrive at the number of trebles, as with the earlier, three-race example:

Races 1 2 and 3 = $2 \times 1 \times 2 = 4$
Races 1 2 and 4 = $2 \times 1 \times 4 = 8$
Races 1 3 and 4 = $2 \times 2 \times 4 = 16$
Races 2 3 and 4 = $1 \times 2 \times 4 = 8$

Total: 36 trebles

Obviously four winners here would guarantee a profit, and three winners at reasonable odds (no worse than 2–1, 2–1 and 3–1 before tax for instance) would recover outlay. Provided the punter gets the relationship between cover and total stake right, avoiding an excess of selections in too many legs, a wager like this enables him to cash in nicely when his reading of form narrows selected races down to just a few 'live' candidates in each.

Fourfolds

Calculations for fourfolds are exactly the same, where four races obviously make one fourfold, five races five fourfolds, six races 15 fourfolds, seven races 35 fourfolds.

Here are a couple of examples:

Race 1:   SAN MARINO
           COME FORTH

Race 2:   FLAMING GLEN
           JUNGLE FOLLY
           IMPLICATED
           MAORI BOY

Race 3:   TOY SHOP
           SAVIC

Race 4:   TANGENT
           SOLID FUEL

           One selection in each race
           $= 2 \times 4 \times 2 \times 2$
           $= 32$ fourfolds

Although 32 bets are involved here, only one of these can win, which suggests very ordinary odds for the most part. But perhaps combined with one winner at a good price it can show a good gain.

This is an illustration of a bet for more races than the basic four:

Race 1:   BRIDGEOVER
           TOM BASKER
Race 2:   GAME VICTORY
           COURT WINGS
Race 3:   CHAMPOO
Race 4:   HORSE POWER
           STARS AND BARS
           QUIET MAN
Race 5:   WAR LEGEND
           NOW AND AGAIN

In this case four from five races make five possible fourfolds and a grand total of bets calculated thus:

$$\text{Races 1 2 3 and 4} = 2 \times 2 \times 1 \times 3 = 12$$
$$\text{Races 1 2 3 and 5} = 2 \times 2 \times 1 \times 2 = 8$$
$$\text{Races 1 2 4 and 5} = 2 \times 2 \times 3 \times 2 = 24$$
$$\text{Races 1 3 4 and 5} = 2 \times 1 \times 3 \times 2 = 12$$
$$\text{Races 2 3 4 and 5} = 2 \times 1 \times 3 \times 2 = 12$$

Total: 68 fourfolds

This combination strategy need not be applied to doubles, trebles or fourfolds separately. A compound wager taking in two, or even all three, components, has lots of potential. A fairly inexpensive version might be:

Race 1:	CUBAN TAN
	WELSH JOKER
Race 2:	AVRO JET
Race 3:	RUM NEWS
	SET TO MUSIC
Race 4:	POET'S SON
	SILK TOWN
	Cover one selection in each race for 18 doubles, 20 trebles and 8 fourfolds

Combination Bets with Reduction Guarantees and Alternatives

Finally, before leaving combination betting, below is a wager of this type which also embraces the principle of reduction guarantees explained in the previous chapter. It allows the punter to cover three horses in each of four races, and reduces the cost of trebles from 108 to just 36 bets. The guarantee is that with four winners there must be at least one winning treble and an outside chance of four. At the same time it is only 2–1 against a winning treble if only three winners are found.

In making an actual bet each horse must first be assigned a letter depending on the race in which it is engaged. The sets of four trebles are then built up by transposition from the schedule.

Race 1: A B C
Race 2: D E F
Race 3: G H I
Race 4: J K L

ADHK	4 trebles
AEIJ	4 trebles
AFGL	4 trebles
BDGJ	4 trebles
BEHL	4 trebles
BFIK	4 trebles
CDIL	4 trebles
CEGK	4 trebles
CFHJ	4 trebles

Total: 36 trebles

Unfortunately the bet has to be written out on nine separate slips, for their is no way of expressing its structure in one simple instruction. However, anyone who is prepared to take some trouble and give this method the chance it deserves could well be rewarded for their labours. With three horses in each race covered, some very big trebles indeed are possible when the selections at the more remunerative end of the odds scale actually win.

Combination bets as a whole are good value for the punter, therefore, but inevitably there will be those who are not comfortable with the wasted stakes that must be accepted as part and parcel of that approach to building up winning cumulative bets. Readers with such reservations might like to consider one final suggestion which still allows backers alternatives in the event of their main fancies being beaten.

Everyone will be familiar with the following tale of woe. You select two good candidates for a bet, but only one wins, whilst the other just fails. You have probably backed both of them to win, but the tasty double at cumulative odds has not materialised. At the same time you see to your chagrin that another horse, one over which you hesitated long and hard, comes home doing the proverbial handsprings. Perhaps another major fancy has won and run unbacked as well. After all, you cannot bet on everything you think will win.

The following pattern of bets could serve as the answer to this old, old story of 'what might have been', from which we must all have suffered at some time.

Two best bets, A and B, are chosen as before. They are still to be backed in a double, but two other horses with good chances in two more races are also selected. They can be called C and D. The final wager becomes:

AB
AC
AD Five doubles
BC
BD

Thus there are alternatives to each of the main fancies, but since all the selections are in different races, there is no wastage of stakes. All five doubles can win. Even if only the basic AB double comes up, reasonable prices will still produce a sound overall profit.

The same can be done with trebles. A and B are again the biggest fancies, but C, D and E are chosen as likely alternatives. Now the bet is:

ABC
ABD
ABE
ACD
ACE   Nine trebles
ADE
BCD
BCE
BDE

Thus if both of the main bets win, there are three additional selections which can make up at least one winning treble and possibly more. If one of them fails, all is not lost. Again there are horses in reserve. And once again the underlying principle of the whole bet is that each of the nine stakes can produce a win with no automatic loss of outlay.

Danger Selections

One final strategy for trebles is to include danger selections to the main fancy in each race rather than additional nominations in other races. Only one of the four trebles involved can win this time, but by using same-race alternatives the punter gives himself excellent and cheap insurance against the annoying scenario of one loser in three that ruins so many ambitious trebles.

Here is the rota of bets:

	Selection	Danger
Race 1	A	D
Race 2	B	E
Race 3	C	F

Four trebles: ABC, ABF, ACE, BCD

Conclusions

This chapter as a whole offers a wide range of plans based specifically on the use of additional selections. If your natural betting inclination is not to put all your eggs in one basket, then there ought to be something in the foregoing pages to appeal to you. Combination bets are not the only way of playing safe at racing, but because big returns for a limited outlay are still possible with them, there is much to be said in their favour from both points of view.

5
Group Betting

Introduction

As was partly explained in Chapter 1 in the discussion on the concept of value, bookmakers bet to figures, and a knowledge of exactly how they do it is essential for the backer, if only because it gives him a proper understanding of just what he is up against in the racing game. But professional gamblers bet to figures too. During their heyday between the World Wars, the legendary 'Old England', Charles Hannam and others successfully applied, in reverse, the bookmakers' own system of fixing the odds, and were able thereby to make a princely income from their betting activities.

Their method of making a 'book' against the 'book' on several horses in the same race which in their opinion held the best chances of winning nearly always involved betting at odds on, and is not really for the ordinary backer who, unlike the professional, cannot operate in the racecourse Ring on a regular basis. Also, these men, along with their arch enemies, the top bookmakers, possessed a lightning facility with odds not given to ordinary mortals. Even so, within limits, the stay-at-home punter of only average mathematical ability can, on occasion, exploit their methods to good advantage.

Bookmakers' Percentages

The first step is to learn how a course bookmaker prices up his board on a race. Reading of form and racecourse 'intelligence' about stable confidence come into it, but the ruling principle in the structuring of a betting market is the price about each runner converted to a percentage. So a horse at Evens has a 50–50 chance of winning or 50 per cent, one at 6–4 a 60–40 chance or 40 per cent, a 3–1 shot is rated 75–25 or 25 per cent, and so on.

The method by which these percentage probabilities are calculated for all odds, including broken prices, is to add 1 point to the 'odds to 1' and divide into 100.

Example: 13–8 represents odds of 13 ÷ 8 = 1.625–1 plus 1 = 2.625; divided into 100 gives a percentage of 38.1, to one place of decimals.

This calculation can be done for every rate of odds to produce a table of percentages which may be consulted at a glance, thus obviating the necessity to do the maths every time.

RACING ODDS EXPRESSED AS A PERCENTAGE

Odds	%	Odds	%	Odds	%
8–15	65.2	9–4	30.8	12–1	7.7
4–7	63.6	95–40	29.6	13–1	7.1
8–13	61.9	5–2	28.6	14–1	6.7
4–6	60.0	11–4	26.7	15–1	6.3
8–11	57.9	3–1	25.0	16–1	5.9
4–5	55.6	100–30	23.1	18–1	5.3
5–6	54.6	7–2	22.2	20–1	4.8
10–11	52.4	4–1	20.0	22–1	4.3
20–21	51.2	9–2	18.2	25–1	3.8
Evens	50.0	5–1	16.7	28–1	3.4
21–20	48.8	11–2	15.4	30–1	3.2
11–10	47.6	6–1	14.3	33–1	2.9
6–5	45.5	13–2	13.3	35–1	2.8
5–4	44.4	7–1	12.5	40–1	2.4
11–8	42.1	15–2	11.8	50–1	2.0
6–4	40.0	8–1	11.1	66–1	1.5
13–8	38.1	17–2	10.5	100–1	1.0
7–4	36.4	9–1	10.0	150–1	0.7
15–8	34.8	19–2	9.5	200–1	0.5
2–1	33.3	10–1	9.1	250–1	0.4
85–40	32.0	11–1	8.3	500–1	0.2

The Bookmakers' Over-Round

Bookmakers know the numbers in this table like the back of their hand, and here is an example of how they would have used them to bet on a little race in the North of England:

Odds	Horse	%
11–10	LOXANDRA	47.6
11–4	MAMNOON	26.7
4–1	LAFTAH	20.0
8–1	SONGS OF INNOCENCE	11.1
25–1	TIAPHENA	3.8
40–1	EDINBURGH REAL ALE	2.4
50–1	CADEAUX PREMIERE	2.0
		113.6

In this case the 'over-round' on a 'round' book of 100 is 13.6 per cent. That is the bookmaker's 'edge' on the race and means that punters as a whole are always betting with him at that rate of disadvantage. The over-round varies from race to race depending on market conditions, but as long as the total of the odds about all the runners in a race converted to percentages exceeds 100, the bookmaker retains a favourable trading margin over his clients.

If, on the other hand, the aggregate of the percentages is less than 100, a punter could back every horse in the race and be certain of a profit. Suppose, for example, the above contest had been priced up as follows:

Odds	Horse	%
6–4	LOXANDRA	40.0
3–1	MAMNOON	25.0
9–1	LAFTAH	10.0
9–1	SONGS OF INNOCENCE	10.0
50–1	TIAPHENA	2.0

50–1	EDINBURGH REAL ALE	2.0
50–1	CADEAUX PREMIERE	2.0
		91.0

Now all an alert backer has to do is to stake according to the percentages to ensure a gain from the race whichever horse is successful:

Stake	Odds	Horse	Return
£40	6–4	LOXANDRA	£100
£25	3–1	MAMNOON	£100
£10	9–1	LAFTAH	£100
£10	9–1	SONGS OF INNOCENCE	£100
£2	50–1	TIAPHENA	£102
£2	50–1	EDINBURGH REAL ALE	£102
£2	50–1	CADEAUX PREMIERE	£102
£91			

The last two returns are not exactly to £100 because of the rounding of the percentages in the table up or down to one place after the decimal point, but it can be seen that for a total outlay of £91, the punter must make a profit of at least £9, whatever the result.

Improving the Backer's Percentages

No bookmaker would actually lay such prices and in the normal course of events when the 'book' is always over-round, the backer cannot 'steal' money in this way. He must always confront the percentage in excess of 100 which ensures that the overall odds on a race are in the bookmaker's favour, not his. What he can do, however, is to take a view based on form as to which horses may win and which have only relatively poor chances, and then construct his own 'book' to give him the advantage if he is correct in his assessment.

Consider this example:

Odds	Horse	%
9–4	PROPHET MASTER	30.8
100–30	TOLANDRO	23.1
9–2	COLONISER	18.2
7–1	PETITE MARCHE	12.5
12–1	PANAWAY	7.7
12–1	WHY ELOPE	7.7
14–1	KIPSANG	6.7
14–1	SANDSHOES	6.7
20–1	GAY GORDON	4.8
33–1	CHINA TIGER	2.9
		121.1

Despite superficial appearances perhaps, this is not a particularly generous 'book' for the punter with an 'over-round' of 21.1 per cent against him. If, for example, he believes that the race can only go to one of the four market leaders, and that the rest of the field has no real chance, then adding up the percentages, he finds that 30.8 + 23.1 + 18.2 + 12.5 = 84.6 per cent. This is the probability of one of these four winning, in the bookmaker's estimation. If the punter was to back them all in the manner illustrated above, he would be betting at a rate of 15.4 per cent to 84.6 per cent, that is at odds of over 5–1 on. With six other horses in the field, clearly such a wager would be a very poor one because the risk is out of all proportion to the potential gain.

If he carries the process of elimination a stage further, he may decide that the race lies between three, not four horses, namely Prophet Master, Coloniser or Petite Marche. Now the aggregate of the percentages is 30.8 + 18.2 + 12.5 = 61.5 per cent. This time he would be betting at around 6–4 on. If he were supremely confident that his analysis of the race was correct, this might well seem a reasonable bet. The bookmaker still holds the whip hand to the tune of 21.1 per cent over the totality of the punters betting on the race as a whole, but in terms of his particular fancies, he can take an acceptable profit on outlay, and like the bookmaker in relation to each individual client, he enjoys the luxury of having more than one horse on his side.

At this point it is instructive to look at how a professional backer might approach this race. He is betting in the Ring and is in a position to exploit the competition for business between the various layers. Expert in reading the signs, the 'pro' steps in early when the favourite is on offer at 11–4. Coloniser is easy to back and although most bookmakers are offering 9–2, 11–2 is readily available with quite a few of them. When the favourite begins to shorten down to 9–4, Petite Marche, originally marked up at no better than 7–1, drifts out to 10–1. Again having read the Ring signals correctly, the 'pro' once again gets the best of the odds and strikes his final bet on the race at that price. The percentage position about the three fancied animals is now:

Odds	Horse	%
11–4	PROPHET MASTER	26.7
11–2	COLONISER	15.4
10–1	PETITE MARCHE	9.1
		51.2

So the professional backer has improved his position by all of 10.3 percentage points, and for someone who makes his living at racing and habitually bets in large sums, this is a big difference. He now has just about even money to his three against the field and the chance of a very good profit.

Nevertheless he can misread market trends too, and for the stay-at-home punter in the local betting shop improving the margin in the above way may not seem all that significant. Nevertheless, properly applied in the right races, this professional method of group betting can be very effective even for the amateur speculator.

For example, the Derby at Epsom is an annual puzzle which most would be less than confident about solving with a single selection. The prices on a recent running for the fancied contenders were as follows:

7–2	ERHAAB
6–1	BROADWAY FLYER
8–1	LINNEY HEAD
10–1	WEIGH ANCHOR
10–1	COLONEL COLLINS
12–1	SUNSHACK
14–1	MISTER BAILEYS
14–1	KING'S THEATRE
16–1	WAITING
20–1	FOYER
33–1	KHAMASEEN
40–1	OTHERS

Suppose three horses are genuinely fancied – Erhaab, King's Theatre and Foyer. The punter wishes to stake £15 before tax on the race as a whole.

The first stage is the conversion of the odds available for each runner to a percentage probability, using the table given earlier:

Odds	Horse	%
7–2	ERHAAB	22.2
14–1	KING'S THEATRE	6.7
20–1	FOYER	4.8

The aggregate of the percentages is 22.2 + 6.7 + 4.8 = 33.7 per cent. One needs to divide the intended £15 outlay by this figure to arrive at a basic betting unit:

$$£15 \div 33.7 = 0.445p$$
$$\text{Betting unit} = 45p$$

The stakes on each horse, therefore, will be:

ERHAAB	22.2 × 45p = £9.99 or £10
KING'S THEATRE	6.7 × 45p = £3.02 or £3
FOYER	4.8 × 45p = £2.16 or £2.10

Following this rota of stakes, the actual winner among the three selections will always produce approximately the same return and the same amount of profit:

Stake	Odds	Horse	Return
£10.00	7–2	ERHAAB	£45.00
£3.00	14–1	KING'S THEATRE	£45.00
£2.10	20–1	FOYER	£44.10
£15.10			

Thus the punter is certain of an overall gain of about £30 before tax if one of his three nominations wins, and in such an open race he might well be justified in considering this a better proposition than risking the whole of his £15 on just one candidate.

As we shall see again in the next chapter, big handicaps such as the Lincoln, the Royal Hunt Cup and the Cambridgeshire offer little 'value' for the professional backer. Nevertheless the man in the street can use the above formula effectively to back a lot of horses and still emerge with a sound gain.

Here is an example of how it could work using, as an example, a recent renewal of one of the biggest betting races of the year, the Wokingham Handicap at Royal Ascot. The fancied horses are:

10–1	POKER CHIP
14–1	NO EXTRAS
20–1	VENTURE CAPITALIST
50–1	CHAMPAGNE GRANDY

Referring to the table, the percentages for each candidate are:

Odds	Horse	%
10–1	POKER CHIP	9.1
14–1	NO EXTRAS	6.7
20–1	VENTURE CAPITALIST	4.8
50–1	CHAMPAGNE GRANDY	2.0
		22.6

Again the stake is to be £15, so that one betting unit will be £15 ÷ 22.6 = 66p. Multiply this by the percentage probability for every selection, and the final wager becomes:

POKER CHIP	9.1 × 66p = £6.01 or £6.00
NO EXTRAS	6.7 × 66p = £4.42 or £4.40
VENTURE CAPITALIST	4.8 × 66p = £3.17 or £3.20
CHAMPAGNE GRANDY	2.0 × 66p = £1.32 or £1.30

The returns will be, given a winning selection:

Stake	Odds	Horse	Return
£6.00	10–1	POKER CHIP	£66.00
£4.40	14–1	NO EXTRAS	£66.00
£3.20	20–1	VENTURE CAPITALIST	£67.20
£1.30	50–1	CHAMPAGNE GRANDY	£66.30
£14.90			

The rounding up or down of the percentages as shown in the table and of the stakes to the nearest 10p produces the slight deviation from the intended £15 outlay and in the rates of return, but should any horse win, there will always be a profit of around £51 before betting tax.

Obviously the wager can be extended to take in more horses in the race, provided some reduction in profit potential is accepted as the price to be paid for extra chances of finding the winner:

Odds	Horse	%
10–1	POKER CHIP	9.1
14–1	NO EXTRAS	6.7
20–1	VENTURE CAPITALIST	4.8
25–1	LORD OLIVIER	3.8
25–1	SHEILA'S SECRET	3.8
50–1	CHAMPAGNE GRANDY	2.0
		30.2

$$£15 \div 30.2 = 0.497$$
Betting unit = 50p

POKER CHIP	9.1 × 50p = £4.55 or £4.50
NO EXTRAS	6.7 × 50p = £3.35 or £3.30
VENTURE CAPITALIST	4.8 × 50p = £2.40
LORD OLIVIER	3.8 × 50p = £1.90
SHEILA'S SECRET	3.8 × 50p = £1.90
CHAMPAGNE GRANDY	2.0 × 50p = £1.00

Stake	Odds	Horse	Return
£4.50	10–1	POKER CHIP	£49.50
£3.30	14–1	NO EXTRAS	£49.50
£2.40	20–1	VENTURE CAPITALIST	£50.40
£1.90	25–1	LORD OLIVIER	£49.40
£1.90	25–1	SHEILA'S SECRET	£49.40
£1.00	50–1	CHAMPAGNE GRANDY	£51.00
£15.00			

Now six horses have been backed, with a profit of around £35 guaranteed if any one of the six wins. Someone playing the ante-post market just a few days before the race could very probably improve this margin considerably by taking advantage of competitive prices which will shorten up on the day of the event.

All in all, even if the average punter is not prepared to embrace group betting as a regular strategy, there will be times when it can prove very rewarding to careful racing fans who like to keep risks down to a minimum.

6

Selection Procedures

Introduction

Mathematical formulae and clever staking can only do so much. To win with any degree of consistency, the punter must also find ways of regularly backing enough winners to allow the systematic arrangement of stakes to work in his favour. Over the years many excellent methods of horse selection have been devised from many quarters, but no one has ever succeeded in finally laying down a set of rules which will automatically guarantee a profit from a given number of selections. If it were otherwise the betting industry as we know it would have ceased to exist. On the other hand, by being ultra selective procedures can be established which MAY, and here the emphasis is on the word 'may', indicate enough winning bets from a series to make an overall gain possible. However, this will most likely be only a percentage of the total outlay, with no absolute certainty of success.

This chapter offers no automatic selection systems with hard and fast rules which eliminate the need for the punter to use his own judgement about which horses to back. Rather it presents a set of conclusions, based on statistics and experience, which in combination add up to a coherent strategy of selection. Racing has many facets, but seven main criteria are considered, and these are the ones which have the greatest bearing on results. Throughout, the object is to point the reader firmly in the right direction when making decisions about the probable outcome of different sorts of races, while steering him away from the common mistakes which many punters habitually make.

Form – Race Ratings

Obviously the 'form' of racehorses must be the most important consideration in the process of selection. Definitions of form are legion but in general terms it can be said to be past running, particularly recent running, that is used as an indicator of probable future performance. This is a vast subject for study but even the most dedicated follower of the sport needs some relatively quick and easy way of assessing how one horse is likely to run in competition with others.

Fortunately nowadays, practically every sporting and national daily newspaper features race ratings, based on private handicaps compiled by journalists who specialise in the field. These are certainly the best measures of form which are readily available, but they must be used sensibly. They all have inherent weaknesses, not least the trap which a lot of inexperienced punters fall into of taking everything at its face value without reading between the lines.

This is where the other factors discussed in this chapter come in, although it is a fact that even by themselves, ratings, especially in non-handicap races, can be a very useful aid to winner-finding. In non-handicaps the weights to be carried are determined, not by the official handicapper intent on giving every runner an equal chance but, by the Weight-for-Age scale, usually with small, additional penalties for previous successes at various levels of competition.

Every horse has more or less the same chance and the ratings given in numerical form in newspapers are a very fair assessment of what a horse has accomplished on the racecourse. Even so there is no guarantee that it will reproduce its known form and run exactly to the figure assigned to it by the compiler of the ratings. In non-handicaps generally the backer should obviously concentrate on the most highly rated horses, but without always expecting the top-rated horse of all to win. Just as important, he should avoid animals rated a long way behind those with the best figures.

The value of form-based race ratings in handicaps is much more questionable. If the backer accepts as the gospel truth the published numerical ratings, he is in fact doing no more than favouring the opinion of one expert over another, that is the assessment of a private handicapper over the view of his official counterpart. The top-rated horse is the one which, in the opinion of the former, is best-in when the figures are compared with the weights actually allotted for a race.

Whilst newspaper ratings are certainly successful, some of the time, in pinpointing a horse which has been officially underestimated on current form, they still need to be treated with caution. As with conditions races, ratings in handicaps are more useful for indicating a small group from which the winner may come, rather than a single candidate apparently holding a decisive weight advantage on form. As a general rule they are most effective when a high rating, indicating a certain level of ability, is accompanied by evidence of very good recent running in similar company. Though it happens much less frequently than in non-handicaps, horses given no chance by the published figures can, and do, win handicap races.

But in the main, private handicaps in the form of race ratings, professionally compiled, provide an excellent quick guide to probable results. For all that, they are still only a guide. The punter who hopes ultimately to be successful must definitely not rely on them alone. Because race ratings can never be the complete answer to his problem, he must be prepared to incorporate assessments derived from other factors into his overall view of likely performance.

Form Figures

Another form of assessment using a numerical approach is based on the study of form figures, that is the record of recent placings which in newspapers appear to the left of the name of each runner, where '1' indicates a win, '2' a second, '3' a third, '4' a fourth, and '0' or any other symbol an unplaced run, with the last-time-out figure given on the extreme right of the row. Many purists would no doubt argue that so simplistic an approach to the complex business of the study of form has little or no value, but the fact remains that many ordinary punters set great store by these figures.

Here two points need to be considered. First, do they in fact have a validity as an indicator of winners. Second, if so, which figures are of the greatest significance?

For the purposes of this book these two questions have been addressed via the medium of an extensive, statistical study, and a number of conclusions have been found to be inescapable and definitely proven.

The main finding was that horses having certain sets of form figures do consistently record more wins than others. Also, these superior figures, even when they fail to herald a win, produce a very high percentage of animals which reach a place.

In addition, three-figure form is much more reliable in both these instances than the now fashionable six-figure row carried by all newspapers in recent years. The reason for this is quite simple. Up-to-date form is always the best guide. Placings achieved four, five and six outings ago have little relevance to the present.

Finally, not only do certain form figures have undeniable value for the selector in non-handicap races, certainly in those where all the contestants have had a good few runs, the best of them also have considerable bearing on handicap events. This is true despite the fact that a run of good performances in races of this type, particularly one or more outright wins, will inevitably see a horse rise in the weights. The one exception to this finding is when a handicapper goes to the well once too often after recording a hat-trick of wins.

For several very good reasons therefore, form figures may be regarded with considerable justification as a sound, shorthand summary of current racing ability and a good indicator of probable winners. However those punters who already employ this approach tend to have widely differing views as to what are the best figures, and the reason for this is almost certainly that their preferences are not based on hard, statistical data.

Here this book fills an important gap, for below are listed those form figures, grouped into six ranks, which according to our comprehensive survey are most indicative of winners. It is also significant that they carry approximately equal weight in all types of race, not just when handicaps are compared with non-handicaps, but across the entire racing spectrum where gradations in the class of runners are extremely various. Also, even though the requirement to jump hurdles and fences in National Hunt racing cuts down the number of animals which actually record the sets of figures given below, they are as potent over the jumps as on the Flat in producing winners.

TOP RANK	111	(Not in handicaps)
	11	(Two career runs only)
SECOND RANK	101	
	131	
THIRD RANK	121	
	112	
FOURTH RANK	211	
	114	

FIFTH RANK	011
SIXTH RANK	311
	321
	122
	21 (Two career runs only)

It is left to the individual to make the best use of this information in his own way, but combined with other recommendations in this chapter, judicious attention paid to the above rankings, if only as one selection factor among several, should assist in the quest for winners.

Betting Forecasts

The betting forecast is intended to give some indication of how the actual betting on a race is likely to go. Market moves can produce considerable variation from a newspaper forecast. Weight of money on the racecourse can alter the expected odds for individual horses quite dramatically, and also change the order in which runners are ranked by the ascending scale of available prices. More often than not, however, the forecasts provided via the Press are remarkably accurate in predicting the make and shape of the final racecourse market on a race.

These betting forecasts are, in a very real sense, an assessment of the chances of at least the leading contenders for a given event, as indeed are the full range of odds offered by bookmakers at the track. The favourite is held to have the best prospects, the second favourite the next best, and so on for each runner whose relative chance is rated by its odds. Consequently there is at least a theoretical case to be made for using newspaper forecasts as an aid to selection, and practice confirms that the punter can draw some positive conclusions from them, taking statistical evidence as his starting point.

Below is a complete breakdown for Flat, for National

Hunt and for All-Weather Flat racing. The statistics show how the indications of the betting forecast fared over the entire British racing programme for a three-year period. The forecast used throughout was that of a leading racing daily.

FLAT – Turf

Stakes and conditions races (two-year-olds)
Favourite	40.9% won
Second favourite	23.1% won
Third favourite	12.8% won
Others	23.2% won

Stakes and conditions races (older horses)
Favourite	38.4% won
Second favourite	22.2% won
Third favourite	17.5% won
Others	21.9% won

Handicaps (all ages)
Favourite	23.4% won
Second favourite	19.9% won
Third favourite	14.2% won
Others	42.5% won

FLAT – All-Weather

Stakes and conditions races (all ages)
Favourite	39.3% won
Second favourite	23.9% won
Third favourite	22.1% won
Others	14.7% won

.

Handicaps (all ages)

Favourite	26.1% won
Second favourite	24.5% won
Third favourite	17.6% won
Others	31.5% won

NATIONAL HUNT

Non-handicap hurdles

Favourite	48.0% won
Second favourite	22.0% won
Third favourite	12.7% won
Others	17.3% won

Non-handicap chases

Favourite	48.0% won
Second favourite	24.4% won
Third favourite	9.4% won
Others	18.2% won

Handicap hurdles

Favourite	27.8% won
Second favourite	25.8% won
Third favourite	15.3% won
Others	31.1% won

Handicap chases

Favourite	37.6% won
Second favourite	23.6% won
Third favourite	12.1% won
Others	26.7% won

These figures are so impressive in a certain sense that no apology is offered for summarising them in a slightly different form:

FIRST THREE IN THE BETTING FORECAST

FLAT – Turf

Stakes and conditions races (two-year-olds)	76.8% won
Stakes and conditions races (older horses)	78.1% won
Handicaps (all ages)	57.5% won

FLAT – All-Weather

Stakes and conditions races (all ages)	85.3% won
Handicaps (all ages)	68.5% won

NATIONAL HUNT

Non-handicap hurdles	82.7% won
Non-handicap chases	81.8% won
Handicap hurdles	68.9% won
Handicap chases	73.3% won

These tables show that every type of non-handicap race under all three codes was dominated by the first three in the forecast. Even in handicaps, reputedly so much more difficult for the backer than conditions races, this group accounted for a significant proportion of the winners, although here there was quite a bit of variation between the three sorts of racing, Flat handicaps on grass showing the lowest percentage of all.

With this one exception, the impression left by all the above figures points to a single, overwhelming fact, namely that in most races *it is pointless to look beyond the first three in the betting forecast for the probable winner.* The punter may, on occasion, decide to depart from this rule, but if he does so, for whatever reason, he should be aware that he is flying in the face of a body of statistical evidence the strength of which is quite unprecedented when it comes to betting on horses.

Backers aiming to find a single selection for a race would have to eliminate two of the three favoured quotes, but in terms of winning percentage alone, the significance of this factor in the search for winners can hardly be underestimated. Also, in acting on this conclusion, it is important to remember that the second and third quoted horses *taken together* often win more races than the first choice in the forecast. In other words backers must not allow themselves to be mesmerised by a favourite for no other reason than that it happens to be the shortest price of the three horses with the best statistical chance.

Handicaps v. Non-handicaps

As we have already noted, in a handicap every horse is supposed to have the same chance. This equality is, however, only theoretical. Quite apart from any mistakes made by the Handicapper, current fitness and the vagaries of form ensure that in most handicaps the runners are strung out down the course just as in any other sort of race.

Also, weight affects different horses in different ways. A big horse is obviously more likely to be able to shrug off a sharp rise in its weight than a small one, whilst there are some racing experts who assert that weight 'off' has a different effect on running to identical weight 'on'. Again, a horse's reaction to fluctuations in the burdens it carries may be as much a matter of psychology as physical conformation.

All these factors are imponderables which are difficult, if not impossible, to measure accurately and tend to make winners much more difficult to spot in handicaps than in conditions races. On the other hand, because of their more open nature, prices for all runners including the favourite are generally better. This provides some justification for betting in races which are almost always harder to analyse.

Despite the complexities inherent in handicaps, it is

clear from the previous section that the first three in the betting forecast are still the most likely to succeed. These are the horses which, in the professional opinion of the compiler, have shown the best recent form and results tend to confirm that this is a sound criterion for winner-finding, at least as a basic rule-of-thumb guide.

However, in handicaps rather than non-handicaps, another sort of horse is frequently given a prominent position in the actual racecourse market. This is the animal which has been performing indifferently in recent outings, but whose return to form is heralded by much shorter odds than a literal interpretation of the form book would allow. Many of these horses win, particularly in Flat handicaps, and statistically account for a lot of winners which fall outside the favoured betting-forecast quotes. For the punter picking out his selections well in advance of racing and indeed for anyone who bases his assessments on public form, such horses are an additional complication which add to the difficulties involved in betting on handicaps.

Trying to pinpoint horses which have been 'tuned up' to show a sudden, dramatic improvement in form after dropping significantly in the weights is one more handicap puzzle for the punter to solve. More will be said of this in the next section, but fitness aside, here are a number of simple guidelines. Used intelligently these should, at the very least, save those who chance their arm in handicaps a great deal of money in losing stakes:

1   Avoid handicaps with big fields. Realistically, unravelling a handicap of maximum of about a dozen runners is the limit of anyone's ability as a form reader.

2   The fact that a horse was down the field last time out is no barrier to success in a handicap. Good recent form is still the best indicator but approach all handicaps

with an open mind. Look for and be prepared for the unexpected.

3   Sprints are much less reliable from a form point of view than races over a distance of ground. Sprint handicappers tend to beat one another with monotonous regularity, making a nonsense of the Form Book. Handicaps over a mile and a half or more, though relatively few in number, consistently see horses with good form near the top of the weights in the winner's enclosure.

4   Among trainers there is no such thing as a 'handicap specialist', despite an unfortunate tendency in the Press to write up, in this way, any handler who has a purple patch. Trainers, like horses, have good runs and bad runs, and all trainers want to win handicaps. Except for an elite few, they are every stable's bread and butter. Some trainers on the other hand do make a speciality of winning handicaps on particular courses. Consistent success of this kind over a number of years is a matter of public record.

5   Never back a horse in a handicap ridden by an apprentice claiming the 7lbs allowance. It is almost always an indication of lack of confidence on the part of connections when an inexperienced 'chalk' jockey is engaged to reduce the poundage to be carried by a highly weighted horse, even though there may be the occasional winning exception that proves the rule. Conversely, the booking of a top jockey by a small stable is a sure sign that a horse is 'expected'.

Each of the above negatives has a positive but in the main most bets should be made in non-handicaps. Even though prices may be lower in the long run all punters stand or fall by a sound percentage of winners. Only bet in handicaps exceptionally when there seems a very good reason to do so. Even then, pre-race logic may well prove an expensive illusion in any race labelled a handicap.

Fitness

Away from professional racing circles fitness in the thoroughbred racehorse is a much misunderstood concept. The amateur racing enthusiast will certainly be helped in his appreciation of form if he has a proper insight into the business of preparing horses for the racecourse.

Initially they are prepared for public performance by careful attention to feeding and diet, supported by slow and fast work to increase muscle power and tone. In the early weeks of a new season, when an animal has done few serious gallops at home, it may well carry an excess of 'condition', a racing euphemism for fat. Once it has been brought to a physical peak by regular exercise and a race or two, however, the overall state of its athletic well-being remains more or less constant for the rest of its active campaign. Occasionally, even when a horse's season is well advanced, it will 'blow' after a race, indicating that it has received only a very light preparation in the training grounds, and that it has been 'let down' after a period of intense activity. By and large though, most racehorses are near to peak physical fitness throughout the racing year. But, this is very far from being the whole story.

As a breed, thoroughbreds potentially have a large fund of nervous energy. That they are 'highly strung' is well known and this nervous energy is the variable which, in the main, determines performance. If their energy reserves are low they will not run as well as if their inner energy is at a high pitch. When an animal is galloped regularly, the nervous energy gradually builds up to a point where it can perform to its maximum capability on the racecourse. When it has been let down on the other hand, it will have done only relatively easy home work, thus causing its reserves of nervous energy to decline, as well as producing some deterioration in physical tone.

Thus the backer seeking to assess a horse's state of 'fitness' is immediately in difficulties, for he is not privy to stable secrets about the progress of inmates, and the evidence of the Form Book is frequently unhelpful, even confusing.

Horses hold their best form, made possible by a peak of physical fitness and nervous energy, for about a month. This period of racing 'mileage' can vary considerably however. A horse which has been brought along very gradually will probably remain at a peak longer than one which has been given a rushed preparation. Even if it is assumed that every horse has undergone the best possible programme of training, the form cycle can vary significantly from the norm in certain animals. The problem for the backer is that he, unlike the trainer, has no real knowledge of the individual characteristics of any horse he is interested in. Nor does he know what kind of preparation it has been given.

Hence it is very difficult for the independent assessor to chart with any degree of accuracy the progress of an animal's 'form wave', to use an old-fashioned expression. A horse wins a couple of races in quick succession for example, then goes out like a light when heavily backed next time it runs. How could the form student have known that the horse was stale, with its reserves of nervous energy temporarily depleted? The answer may well be that not even the trainer himself was able to assess accurately the fine line between his charge being at its peak or just 'over the top'.

What of the huge number of animals which are repeatedly run when short of the gallop that brings them to their peak until their trainers are satisfied that they can win off their current handicap mark? How can the backer divine when the horse is finally 100 per cent fit? Also, can even the cleverest trainer ever be certain that his timing is exactly right?

Horses are not machines, and gambling trainers, as well as punters, and even the handlers of horses due to run in a Classic race, must accept the fact. However, there is a simple test that the student of form can apply and though it cannot help him to form definite conclusions about the beginning and end of the 'form wave', it will provide a reasonable indication of whether a horse is likely to reproduce good recent form.

Below are the results of a survey covering 500 races on the Flat and 500 for National Hunt racing taken at a time when the season in question was in full swing. It classifies each set of 500 winners according to how many days had elapsed since their immediately previous public outing:

FLAT – 500 races

Winners running within:

1–7 days	21.6%
8–14 days	25.3%
15–21 days	19.2%
22–28 days	20.7%
29+ days	13.2%

NATIONAL HUNT – 500 races

Winners running within:

1–7 days	25.8%
8–14 days	25.4%
15–21 days	18.9%
22–28 days	19.4%
29+ days	10.5%

Since 86.8 per cent of the Flat races were won by horses reappearing within 28 days of their previous run, it is possible to formulate a '28-day-rule' – no horse should be backed if more than 28 days have elapsed since its last racecourse appearance. To make this into an absolute rule might be going too far, but certainly any horse that has been off the track for more than about a month must be treated with the greatest caution.

Similarly for National Hunt racing, a 28-day rule could also be applied, but in this branch of the sport where fitness is vital over the longer distances involved and because of the necessity to jump obstacles, it is worth noting that a '14-day rule' would have yielded no fewer than 51.2 per cent of the jump winners in the survey.

These considerations are a positive aid to finding winners. The only type of race in which they are of very little value, as a matter of course, are Group 1 and 2 contests involving the cream of the horses of each generation. With these animals the four-week 'form wave' does not apply, at least in so far as public performances are concerned. Aimed for just a few top races each season, the best horses are delivered to the racecourse to compete in the Classics and the like at a peak of physical and nervous fitness every time, or at least that is what their trainers hope and believe. They know that all horses have a low 'mileage' and bring their best animals to a peak at home, thus avoiding too many exhausting contests at the highest level on the racecourse.

Trainer Form

In the last few years there has been an explosion of statistics of every kind about racing available to the enthusiast who is keen to study the sport in depth. It is now realised that in many ways human beings are a more reliable factor than horses. Unlike the performance of thoroughbreds which can vary greatly from race to race, and often for no apparent reason, the men and women responsible for their preparation and placing in races are in the main highly consistent in their methods. Hence, the modern preoccupation with trainers' records which, in the case of certain experts, amounts to an alternative that transcends the conventional assessment of form as a way of picking out which horses to back. This section stops a long way short of embracing such a radical approach but there can be no doubt that the punter can draw many valuable lessons from an intimate knowledge of 'trainer form'.

Under all codes of racing, Flat and jumps, there are many trainers, but season after season a small group of handlers regularly do much better than the rest. This is due, above all, to their skill at their chosen profession which attracts to their yards the best horses from the most committed owners with the financial means to breed, or to buy from the available pool of bloodstock, those animals most likely to succeed on the racecourse.

In a recent Flat season for example, the top 12 trainers in the numerical winning list sent out between them no fewer than 957 winners. This comes to about one-fifth of the races run in Britain during that period. Similarly over the jumps the top 12 stables accounted for no less than 891 winners in a single National Hunt season. There are slightly less jump than Flat races during a season, and there are many more trainers operating under winter rules, including the large army of permit holders. Therefore, 891 winners is a very impressive record of achievement for just a small group of yards.

Winning percentages vary from over 25 to under 15, but what is important here is the sheer volume of successes notched up by the top echelon of the training establishment. Leaving aside the form of the horses themselves, it must make sense for the backer to concentrate on the charges of the leading trainers, for they will always have a head start, statistically, over runners from other stables.

There may be occasions when there are grounds for looking beyond the small training clite, but as a general approach there is a lot to be said for mentally upgrading the chance of any horse trained by one of the most successful handlers in terms of wins, the more so as the percentage strike rate of their rivals is no better and in most cases a great deal worse than theirs.

This is particularly true in Flat non-handicaps. In this area the top yards are able to achieve their huge haul of winners year after year because they have a virtual monopoly of the better class horses which can easily be exploited in stakes and conditions races. In handicaps on the other hand, the equalisation of chances by weight has the effect of neutralising their privileged position. Make no mistake, in any race that is not a handicap, trainers of the calibre of Henry Cecil, John Dunlop, John Gosden, Richard Hannon, Michael Stoute and several others have a priceless advantage, and any backer who ignores the fact does so at his peril.

Effect of the Draw

In some races on some courses the effect of the draw cannot be exaggerated. The results of certain sprints, and even of contests up to a mile in distance, can be greatly influenced by a good draw, with those badly drawn having virtually no chance.

On the other hand it would be wrong to make too much of this factor at many venues where the starting positions of runners only marginally influence results, and in some cases not at all. Also, ground conditions and the position of the stalls can often play havoc with preconceived notions about what constitutes a favourable draw.

Below is a short list of courses and distances where this factor in the circumstances given always has a vital role to play. In every case big fields obviously magnify the advantage to a well-drawn animal.

Draw Advantage

High

Beverley:	5f, in any ground.
Chepstow:	5f, in any ground.
Hamilton:	5f–6f, especially in soft ground.
Redcar:	5f, especially in soft ground.
Sandown:	5f, especially in soft ground.
Thirsk:	5f–6f, especially in soft ground.

Low

Chester:	up to one mile in any ground, given a fast break.
Pontefract:	5f–6f, in any ground.
Salisbury:	5f–7f, especially in soft ground.
York:	5f–7f, only in soft ground.

In addition, on certain courses the draw can be absolutely crucial in deciding the outcome of races, but this can vary from season to season, usually due to ground conditions. Races with big fields on the straight courses at Ayr, Doncaster and Goodwood in particular fall into this category. Here the backer is recommended to study the bias as the meeting develops before drawing any definite conclusions about a decisive, prevailing trend.

For as long as organised racing and betting have taken place, indeed long before that, horses in competition have regularly made fools of men. A racehorse is not a robot and will not always do what is expected of it. Nevertheless, form allied to a strong dash of commonsense is still the punter's best means of attack and defence in the battle with the bookmaker. Experience and flair come into it too, but it is hoped that this chapter will have provided some immediate insights that would otherwise have taken many years to acquire through trial and error. And perhaps, not even then!

7

Racing Systems

A System for the English Classics

In the early 1960s a number of racing scribes, writing in several different publications, began to call attention to what was heralded as 'the system that always wins' or put another way, 'the system that never loses'. It seems that they had stumbled on the fact that every year for a century or more, with just a very occasional exception, at least one favourite had won an English Classic in the course of a season. However limited in scope, here was a system to 'beat the book'. A staking plan was attached and the idea enthusiastically written up as a goldmine for punters.

Double up on Classic favourites every year, so the argument went, and a profit was always there for the taking. True enough of course, except that an odds-on chance at the wrong place in the sequence can still produce a loss, even if the condition of one winning favourite per year is fulfilled.

Since then, tradition being the ruling canon of English racing, things have gone on pretty much as before, and only very, very rarely has the minimum standard of one winning Classic favourite out of five not been met.

Readers might well object that up to five bets a year and a single winner – for clearly there can be no more bets after one win in the sequence has been recorded – adds up to a swallow which is hardly likely to make a racing fan's summer. Even so, a detailed examination of the idea will serve very well as an introduction to this chapter on automatic racing systems, that is betting procedures which generate selections from a set of strict rules and which call for no judgement, or very little, on the part of the operator.

Below is a ten-year review of the performance of this system for the Classics. It has been divided into two parts. The first is a grid showing the winning frequency of Classic favourites for five consecutive years in the late eighties and early nineties and it gives a good idea what to expect each year. The most recent season is shown on the right. The second part gives an exact profit and loss account which could have been achieved by anyone working the plan in the following five years.

PERFORMANCE OF CLASSIC FAVOURITES OVER A FIVE-YEAR PERIOD

Classic	Year 1	Year 2	Year 3	Year 4	Year 5
1000 Guineas (Newmarket, May)	WON	WON	—	WON	WON
2000 Guineas (Newmarket, May)	—	WON	WON	—	—
Derby (Epsom, June)	WON	—	WON	—	—
Oaks (Epsom, June)	—	WON	WON	WON	—
St Leger (Doncaster, September)	WON	—	WON	—	WON

Quite apart from demonstrating the high incidence of winning favourites in the Classics – in statistical terms any favourite in any Classic is marginally more likely to win than lose, irrespective of its starting price – the grid shows quite clearly that the idea behind 'the system that always wins' has indeed the potential to turn up a profit with a regularity which is highly unusual in the risky business of backing horses.

Now here is the pre-tax financial record to an opening stake of £10 for the following five years using the pre-planned rota of bets listed below:

1000 Guineas	£10 Win	FAVOURITE (unnamed)
2000 Guineas	£20 Win	FAVOURITE (unnamed)
Derby	£40 Win	FAVOURITE (unnamed)
Oaks	£80 Win	FAVOURITE (unnamed)
St Leger	£160 Win	FAVOURITE (unnamed)

FINANCIAL PERFORMANCE OF BETTING ON CLASSIC FAVOURITES OVER A FIVE-YEAR PERIOD

Year 6

1000 Guineas	Lost	–£10.00
2000 Guineas	Lost	–£20.00
Derby	Lost	–£40.00
Oaks	Lost	–£80.00
St Leger	Won 7–4	+£280.00
	Profit	+£130.00

Year 7

1000 Guineas	Lost	–£10.00
2000 Guineas	Won 5–6	+£16.60
	Profit	+£6.60

Year 8

1000 Guineas	Lost	–£10.00
2000 Guineas	Lost	–£20.00
Derby	Won 7–2	+£140.00
	Profit	+£110.00

Year 9

2000 Guineas	Lost	−£10.00
(Run first in the sequence)		
1000 Guineas	Lost	−£20.00
Oaks	Lost	−£40.00
(Run before the Derby)		
Derby	Lost	−£80.00
St Leger	Won 100–30	+£532.80
	Profit	+£382.80

Year 10

2000 Guineas	Lost	−£10.00
1000 Guineas	Won 10–11	+£18.20
	Profit	+£8.20

Despite the variability in outlay and returns, the result of where winners fall in the sequence and their starting prices, the system produced the expected profit every year. Nothing here to guarantee a life of comfort for the rest of your days, but 'a profit is a profit' as every racing fan and stockbroker will tell you.

The Cup Races and the Sprint Championship

There are a couple of other natural big-race series in the Flat Calendar which lend themselves to application of the idea, namely the five Cup races for stayers and the Sprint Championship made up of the only five Group races in the season over the minimum five-furlong trip. Let us see what happens when the Classic system is extended to them.

There follows a grid for years one to five of a decade of monitoring the long distance Cup series.

PERFORMANCE OF FAVOURITES IN CUP RACES OVER A FIVE-YEAR PERIOD

Cup Race	Year 1	Year 2	Year 3	Year 4	Year 5
Yorkshire Cup (York, May)	WON	WON	WON	WON	—
Gold Cup (Royal Ascot, June)	—	WON	WON	—	—
Goodwood Cup (Goodwood, July)	WON	WON	—	WON	—
Doncaster Cup (Doncaster, September)	—	WON	WON	—	—
Jockey Club Cup (Newmarket, October)	—	WON	WON	—	WON

Once again a preponderance of winning favourites over losers makes the system a potential winner, and so it proved in the following five seasons.

FINANCIAL PERFORMANCE OF BETTING ON
FAVOURITES IN CUP RACES OVER A FIVE-YEAR PERIOD

Year 6

Yorkshire Cup	Won 100–30Jt	+£11.65
	Profit	+£11.65

Year 7

Yorkshire Cup	Lost	–£10.00
Gold Cup	Lost	–£20.00
Goodwood Cup	Lost	–£40.00
Doncaster Cup	Won 5–4	+£100.00
	Profit	+£30.00

Year 8

Yorkshire Cup	Lost	–£10.00
Gold Cup	Lost	–£20.00
Goodwood Cup	Lost	–£40.00
Doncaster Cup	Won 7–2	+£280.00
	Profit	+£210.00

Year 9

Yorkshire Cup	Won 11–4	+£27.50
	Profit	+£27.50

Year 10

Yorkshire Cup	Lost	–£10.00
Gold Cup	Lost	–£20.00
Goodwood Cup	Lost	–£40.00
Doncaster Cup	Won Evens	+£80.00
	Profit	+£10.00

However, the five-year grid for the Sprint Championship gives the first clue that you should not mortgage your house to finance this, or indeed any racing system, whatever past statistics may suggest.

PERFORMANCE OF FAVOURITES IN THE SPRINT CHAMPIONSHIP OVER A FIVE-YEAR PERIOD

Sprint	Year 1	Year 2	Year 3	Year 4	Year 5
Palace House Stakes (Newmarket, May)	—	WON	WON	WON	WON
Temple Stakes (Sandown, May)	—	—	—	—	WON
King's Stand Stakes (Royal Ascot, July)	—	—	WON	—	WON
King George Stakes (Goodwood, July)	—	WON	—	WON	—
Nunthorpe Stakes (York, August)	—	WON	WON	WON	—

Leaving aside comment on the completely blank year for the moment, the financial record for the following five years is summarised below:

FINANCIAL PERFORMANCE OF BETTING ON
FAVOURITES IN CUP RACES OVER A FIVE-YEAR PERIOD

Year 6

Palace House Stakes	Lost	−£10.00
Temple Stakes	Lost	−£20.00
King's Stand Stakes	Won 7–2Jt	+£50.00
	Profit	+£20.00

Year 7

Palace House Stakes	Lost	−£10.00
Temple Stakes	Lost	−£20.00
King's Stand Stakes	Lost	−£40.00
King George Stakes	Won 13–8	+£130.40
	Profit	+£60.40

Year 8

Palace House Stakes	Won 7–2	+£35.00
	Profit	+£35.00

Year 9

Palace House Stakes	Lost	−£10.00
Temple Stakes	Won 10–11	+£18.20
	Profit	+£8.20

Year 10

Palace House Stakes	Lost	−£10.00
Temple Stakes	Won 7–2	+£70.00
	Profit	+£60.00

As with the Classics and the Cup Races, another five years of profit.

The small punter may look askance at some of the stakes required to achieve the above gains, but the fact remains that in 15 sample seasons, a profit accrued on every occasion.

In the remainder of the Group 1, Group 2 and Group 3 programmes on the Flat there are no natural sequences like the above, although similar winning percentages for favourites can be expected overall. Some readers might like to try their hand at dividing the Group programme up into sets of five, and betting in the recommended manner on each separate series.

Another alternative might be to pick out in advance from the weekly racing programme five-race sequences of non-handicaps which, statistically, have an excellent record for favourites. Saturday would be the best day for such an approach – on other days there would seldom be enough meetings with suitable races on which to operate. Staking down the series in chronological order in a betting shop, should lead more often than not to some sort of profit.

Such a series, however well chosen, may fail from time to time. Someone adopting the above £10 rota of stakes would lose £10 plus £20 plus £40 plus £80 plus £160 – £310 at a single stroke. The same is true of the Classic, Cup and Sprint Championships as can be seen in the first season of the Sprint grid. However well things have worked out in the past, there can never be a guarantee, only a probability, of similar success in the future, and a great many winning sequences would be needed to offset the disastrous cost of a single losing series.

This is the objection to all automatic racing systems. Leaving the risky doubling-up staking procedure out of the argument, any method, even one which has a brilliant record in previous years, can suddenly fail for no reason that can be foreseen in advance. In other words, gambling can never be taken out of betting on horses. In fact, in spite of a decade of monitoring and analysing results, the following season saw the failure of both the Cup and Sprint race sequences, although the system did produce its usual winning Classic favourite. It was as if the racing fates were conspiring to issue a warning against complacency. There could be no more telling reminder of the very real dangers that attend all betting systems.

A Plan for Four-Year-Olds

Taking a further example, the following simple little plan usually shows a profit most years. It is based on the six big handicaps which are featured in the last third of the Flat season every year. The idea is to list three-year-olds which win or are placed second, third or fourth in these events, and to back them in their races in the opening weeks of their four-year-old season, ceasing operations at the end of the York meeting in May. Three-year-olds that have run well in big handicap company at the back-end of one season must be live propositions when reappearing in the Spring of the next.

The record for three seasons is analysed below.

PERFORMANCE OF THREE-YEAR-OLD HANDICAPPERS IN THEIR EARLY FOUR-YEAR-OLD CAREERS

Handicap	Three-year-olds in first four places	Results as a four-year-old up to York's May meeting
Season One		
Ebor Handicap	KEY TO MY HEART	Lost, Lost, Won 16–1
Ayr Gold Cup	No qualifier	
Cambridgeshire	HASTEN TO ADD	Did not race
Cesarewitch	RITTO	Won 7–2, Lost
Labroke Autumn Handicap	CAMBARA SHINTILLO	Did not race Lost
November Handicap	SAFETY IN NUMBERS	Won 100–30, Won 7–2

Profit before tax: 22⅙ points

Season Two		
Ebor Handicap	No qualifier	
Ayr Gold Cup	DARING DESTINY ALZIANAH	Lost, Won 15–8 Lost, Lost
Cambridgeshire	HALLING WILLIAM TELL	Did not race Did not race
Cesarewitch	NEW REPUTATION	Lost
Labroke Autumn Handicap	BILLY BUSHWACKER	Won 7–2
November Handicap	SAXON MAID	Did not race

Profit before tax: 1⅚ points

Season Three		
Ebor Handicap	SANMARTINO	Won Evens, Lost
Ayr Gold Cup	STOLEN KISS	Won 12–1, Lost, Lost
Cambridgeshire	CAP JULICA	Did not race
Cesarewitch	NANTON POINT	Did not race
Labroke Autumn Handicap	TARAWA DELTA SOLEIL	Won 10–1, Won 5–4 Lost, Lost
November Handicap	SNOW PRINCESS SECRET SERVICE	Did not race Lost, Lost

Profit before tax: 17¼ points

In two years out of three therefore, this plan yielded a really handsome profit on outlay from a small number of qualifiers and an even smaller number of actual runners.

But what is really significant is the other year, SEASON TWO where winners were in a minority to losers and there was no long-priced winner to carry the system.

Even the best of the automatic racing systems exhibit this tendency with good years followed by one or more bad or indifferent years. Since the percentage of winners to losers and the starting price of winners cannot be predicted in advance, there is no guarantee that a racing system, however good, will go on producing profits season after season. True, the very small number of bets in the three-year-old/four-year-old system has the probable effect of magnifying the possibility of sharp variations from one betting period to another, but even in the case of plans involving many more seasonal bets, swings in profitability are the inevitable consequence of the uncertainties built into the racing game.

A Plan for the Cheltenham Festival

These points are well illustrated again in the third and final example of what can happen to a fundamentally sound racing system. Here things go disastrously wrong.

The two-day National Hunt weekend meeting at Kempton in late February which features the Racing Post Trophy on the Saturday has, for a number of years, been a key indicator for results at the Cheltenham National Hunt Festival a fortnight later. Any horse that runs well at the former meeting should be watched closely at the latter. Translating this into a system, Kempton winners are listed and then backed to win if they run at Cheltenham.

This is the complete three-year record for the plan in recent years:

PERFORMANCE OF KEMPTON FEBRUARY WINNERS AT THE CHELTENHAM FESTIVAL

Season One

Kempton Winner	Cheltenham Result
TOP SPIN	Lost
TEAPLANTER	Lost
HONEST WORD	Lost
BIBENDUM	Lost
ELAINE TULLY	Lost
CLOGHANS BAY	—
BALASANI	Won 9–2
JAZILAH	—
REMITTANCE MAN	Lost
MYSILV	Won 2–1
MONSIEUR LE CURE	Won 15–2
ANTONIN	Won 4–1
MASTER OATS	—
PUNTERS OVERHEAD	—

Profit before tax: 12 points

Season Two

Kempton Winner	Cheltenham Result
BEAR CLAW	Won 3–1
COOL RELATION	—
THE FROG PRINCESS	—
BIG MATT	Lost
HOPS AND POPS	—
FIRED EARTH	Lost
BALANAK	Lost
THUMBS UP	Lost
BRIEF GALE	Won 13–2
GREENBACK	Lost
VAL D'ALENE	Lost
CYBORGO	Lost
MAITRE DE MUSIQUE	Lost

Profit before tax: 1½ points

Season Three

Kempton Winner	Cheltenham Result
DECIDE YOURSELF	—
BUTTERCUP JOE	Lost
COOL DAWN	Lost
SILVERFOOT LAD	Lost
SUPER TACTICS	—
CALL EQUINAME	Lost
ERCKULE	—
ALDERBROOK	Lost
KIMANICKY	Lost
VIKING FLAGSHIP	Lost
DRABORGIE	Lost
ZABADI	Lost
ROUGH QUEST	Lost
SEE ENOUGH	Lost
JOHN DRUMM	Lost

Loss before tax: 12 points

Thus, in the space of three years, what appeared to be a sound betting scheme went from a really good profit in the first year to an indifferent one in the second and to a thumping loss in the third.

What went wrong? Historically the answer is that in the final year no less than five of the Kempton winners ran second at the Cheltenham Festival. That suggests that the plan is fundamentally a good one and this failure notwithstanding, has a sporting chance of yielding a profit in future seasons. Certainly anyone betting at the Festival could do a lot worse than this for a method of sorting out which horses to back, possibly preferring to concentrate on the Kempton winners from the Saturday programme which is of a much higher standard than that of the opening day of the meeting. Though the number of bets will be reduced, this could well be the backer's best option.

The fact remains, however, that the basic Kempton/

Cheltenham plan displayed in just three years, characteristics typical of practically all automatic racing systems of any worth. It showed variable results from one betting period to another with no guarantee of certain success in the future, however good things might have been in the past.

Readers have been warned, but at the risk of being accused of inconsistency, below is a selection of betting plans which system enthusiasts might find interesting. Some people find the discipline of a system useful when betting, and the point about all the methods which follow is that, with but one exception, all of them call for judgement in their application.

Form Horses in Late Summer and Early Autumn

This is a plan for the specialist who takes his betting very seriously indeed and who only gets involved when everything seems in his favour, although obviously its use does not preclude following other methodologies, either simultaneously or at other times.

It is used for only three months of the year, the three months when the normal bias in horse racing is reversed and conditions favour, not the bookmaker, but the backer. These three months are July, August and September – July and August on the Flat, and August and September over the jumps.

Up to July Flat form is variable in the extreme. Fitness is hard to assess early in the season. As competition hots up in May and June, bigger fields and the gradual appearance of better class animals tend to produce reversals in form and plenty of shock results. During July and August on the other hand, form is much more settled. Also, fast ground produces small fields. Form horses starting favourite go in with pleasing regularity in certain kinds of races. Come September however, the situation changes again. The going eases, fields swell and many horses have gone off the boil with too much racing and are at a serious disadvantage against late maturing, autumn types. Form once more becomes unreliable and inconsistent.

August and September similarly are the backers' months in National Hunt racing. By August the new jumping season is well under way, but only a few jumpers can really handle the firm ground. The result is small fields dominated by fit horses which have conditions ideal for them. Starting prices are on the short side but four or five winning favourites at a meeting is a commonplace event. In October the jumping season 'proper' starts. There should have been enough rain to allow the genuine winter types to make their bow and, therefore, the pendulum swings back to the bookmaker with the beginning of the long haul of intense competition which leads up to Cheltenham in March.

In July this system operates on the Flat only. August allows a mixture of bets from both codes of racing. In September selections come exclusively from the jumping sphere.

Three horses a day are selected and backed in three singles, three doubles and a treble in a daily seven-point wager. All selections are drawn from non-handicaps, and only market horses with a clear form advantage are good enough. Within reason the backer should not shy away from the inclusion of some odds-on chances. The aim is to land three winners in a day for successful doubles, crowned by a treble, and winners are more important than prices. On the Flat it is a good idea to ignore the principal meeting of the day if there are plenty of opportunities elsewhere. Generally speaking it is easier to find winners at lowly Thirsk or Yarmouth than at glamorous York or Ascot, just as the likes of Sedgefield and Newton Abbot offer relatively easy pickings for the discerning student of National Hunt form at the appropriate time of year.

The mathematics of the plan are straightforward enough. Around 50 per cent of winners each week should see the bet holding its own overall and, given the circumstances governing selections, such a percentage is easily within reach of any competent racing enthusiast. Profits will accrue from those days when all three selections win. If the operator of the plan can turn up an average of only one successful treble each week, he ought to be well in pocket at the end of the three months of betting.

The system is subject to the vicissitudes of horse racing like any other gamble on the sport, but it is a low risk 'bread and butter' plan. For the patient punter who is prepared to hammer away at this particular chink in the bookmakers' armour, there may be plenty of 'jam' too.

A Plan for Doubles

As we have seen in an earlier chapter, most non-handicaps are won by either the first, second or third favourite. If that is a fact which applies to most races of this type, it certainly applies to any one race, and the chances of the winners of two races taken together coming from this group are only marginally less in statistical terms. This is the germ of a good doubles plan.

The doubles possibilities are as follows:

Race 1	Favourite with	Favourite with	Favourite with
Race 2	Favourite	2nd Favourite	3rd Favourite
Race 1	2nd Favourite with	2nd Favourite with	2nd Favourite with
Race 2	Favourite	2nd Favourite	3rd Favourite
Race 1	3rd Favourite with	3rd Favourite with	3rd Favourite with
Race 2	Favourite	2nd Favourite	3rd Favourite

If favourites win more often than second favourites which in turn succeed more frequently than third favourites, then the statistical probability must be that certain of the above nine combinations are much more likely to win than others.

In betting terms it is suggested that these combinations offer the best prospects of striking a winning double:

Race 1	Favourite
Race 2	Favourite
Race 1	Favourite
Race 2	2nd Favourite
Race 1	Favourite
Race 2	3rd Favourite
Race 1	2nd Favourite
Race 2	Favourite
Race 1	3rd Favourite
Race 2	Favourite

If the clever backer can pick the right races, there are excellent medium-to-long-term prospects of a sound profit by exploiting the above pattern. The trick is to choose horses at reasonable prices in races where the rest of the field beyond the first three in the market appear to have no chance. There will not be two opportunities every racing day, but for the backer who is prepared to wait for it, every now and then a golden chance will come along.

Take this example:

Race 1	11–8, 2–1, 3–1
Race 2	13–8, 7–2, 5–1

**POSSIBLE RETURNS FROM FIVE £1 DOUBLES =
£5 PLUS 45P TAX STAKED.**

	Odds		Returns	Profit
11–8	and	13–8	£6.26	£0.81
11–8	and	7–2	£10.71	£5.26
11–8	and	5–1	£14.28	£8.83
2–1	and	13–8	£7.89	£2.44
3–1	and	13–8	£10.52	£5.07

Thus with two favourites at just over odds against and the
rest of the prices in betting proportion, any winning
combination produces a profit of some sort. Inevitably
there will be losing races too and these must be accepted as
a fact of betting life to be offset against winning days. Over
a reasonable betting period, however, the keen form
student should be able to pick and choose to the extent
that it is highly probable that the market leaders will
include the winners of the two races selected. If he can also
cut out races where there is likely to be an odds-on
favourite, a minimum of one winning favourite will nearly
always pick up a reasonable gain.

Skill and patience are needed to work this plan but it has
statistics on its side and in the right hands can be a money
spinner. Obviously it can be worked on the Flat or over the
jumps.

Flat Handicap Doubles

A similar plan for handicaps concentrates on races with
only six or seven runners and a weak favourite. The
system bet is the second and third favourites in four
doubles. Again skill is needed in the application of the
plan, but it is capable of landing doubles of up to 40–1 for
only a small outlay. The method seems to work best on the
Flat where handicap favourites succeed less often and
there are no fallers to spoil the party.

Top Weights Plan for The Flat

It is a statistical fact that horses near the top of the weights predominate in two types of Flat handicap, namely races over the minimum trip of five furlongs and in contests of two miles or more. Between these two extremes winners come from all points in the weight range.

Taking the first four, five or six runners from the top of the handicap depending on the size of the field in five-furlong or two miles and over races, the backer has a small group which ought to include the eventual winner. He can then make an informed choice based on form and the betting market. The betting is generally a fair indicator in both types of race which feature specialists running over their best distances. As for form, consistency represented by good win-and-place performances in each of the last three or four runs provides a vital clue about staying animals likely to go close. Sprinters however, tend to beat one another from race to race, so don't be put off by a form line of indifferent recent runs. The ability to win is important though, and a potential sprint winner should have got its head in front at least once in its last four or five races.

Doubles Plan for Chases

This little plan aims to exploit the high incidence of winning favourites in three-mile chases, both handicaps and non-handicaps, which is a feature of the winter months, particularly in small fields.

The bet is as follows:

3m NON-HANDICAP CHASE – Favourite
3m HANDICAP CHASE – Favourite and 2nd Favourite
Two win doubles

As for earlier plans for doubles, great care must be exercised in the choice of races and favourites that are likely to start at odds-on in the non-handicap chase should be avoided. But, if two or three good opportunities can be located each week, a decent long-term profit may well accrue from this simple but highly effective method.

Form Plan for Jumpers

For those who like a spot of arithmetic and are content to rely on an automatic guide to finding winners, the following system has yielded consistent gains over the years. In five recent seasons it has never shown a debit balance, and on one occasion produced a profit of just over 60 points.

1 Bet on all races under National Hunt rules in Britain from the beginning of November to the Saturday before the Cheltenham Festival in March.

2 Bet only in non-handicaps.

3 Assess runners according to the following scale applied to their three latest public outings:

WIN	– 1 point
SECOND	– 2 points
THIRD	– 3 points
FOURTH	– 4 points
UNPLACED or failed to finish	– 5 points

4 Only the following qualify for a bet:
   a) Horses with a score of 9 or less in their last three outings.
   b) First or second last time out.
   c) Running within 28 days of their last outing.
   d) From a stable which is currently among the top 20 yards based on the most winners to date. (Early in the season take the top 20 trainers from the previous National Hunt season.)

Conclusions

In the final analysis the business of making racing and betting pay depends on the exercise of flair and judgement. Automatic racing systems can be dangerous in the wrong hands for, whatever the past and present portents, they can never be absolutely relied upon to deliver the goods. But then nor can flair and judgement, and there is no doubt that the regime of following some organised system of betting can help many punters to chart their way through the betting minefield. There is room therefore for both approaches. This chapter will obviously be of most interest to systemites. It is hoped that they will use the knowledge gained from it wisely and well.

8

Twelve Golden Rules of Successful Betting

1. Always Read Your Bookmaker's Rules

Every bookmaker, whether one of the High Street giants or the small, independent operator round the corner, has a set of rules which governs all his transactions with his clients.

If you already patronise one layer and have not been through his 'book of words' with a fine-tooth comb, remedy the defect at once. Equally, if starting to invest with a new firm, at least check how the type of bets you favour will be settled *before* having a bet. This applies particularly to punters who like to bet win and place, or who indulge in fancy conditional bets with, for example, elements of 'any-to-come' or 'stop-at-a-win'.

2. If You Bet at Odds-on, Back the Horse Not the Price

'Never bet at odds-on' is definitely bad advice. What is the difference between 10–11 and Evens? Only one of degree, that's all. On the other hand, consistently trying to 'buy money' with odds-on chances for no other reason than they are odds-on is asking for trouble. Too many get beaten, a lot more than people realise.

But there is another consideration. A number of major statistical surveys, taking in results of whole seasons, have demonstrated quite unequivocally that *random* betting on short-priced animals will always yield a better result for the punter than regularly backing horses at longer odds, and the shorter the odds of fancied horses, the more this is so.

There is nothing wrong with laying the odds therefore, but what is more important is that you genuinely fancy the horse, not just its price which makes it look a good thing. The racecourse test frequently reveals that it was anything but a certain winner.

3. Keep Each-Way Bets to a Minimum

The place element of an each-way bet favours the bookmaker, not the backer. This is demonstrated by the table below which shows the true mathematical odds for each of the four standard categories of each-way wager when compared with the bookmaker's price. The theoretical assumption behind the calculations is that every horse has a mathematically equal chance, and the minimum allowable number of runners in each category is taken, as here the backer has the best theoretical chance.

MATHEMATICAL ODDS FOR EACH-WAY BETS ON REPRESENTATIVE RACES

Race and Odds	True Place Odds	Bookmaker's Price	Advantage to Bookmaker
5 runners ¼ the odds on 1st and 2nd	3 against 2 or 1.50–1	¼ of 4–1 or Evens	+0.50–1
8 runners ⅕ the odds on 1st, 2nd and 3rd	5 against 3 or 1.67–1	⅕ of 7–1 or 1.40–1	+0.27–1
12 runners (Handicaps only) ¼ the odds on 1st, 2nd or 3rd	9 against 3 or 3–1	¼ of 11–1 or 2.75–1	+0.25–1
16 runners (Handicaps only) ¼ the odds on 1st, 2nd, 3rd and 4th	12 against 4 or 3–1	¼ of 15–1 or 3.75–1	−0.75–1

So only in the last category where the backer has 12 horses

against him and four for him, are the place odds in his favour. The true place odds are 12 ÷ 4 or 3–1, but the bookmaker will pay a quarter of 15–1, the true mathematical chance of the backer finding the winner, that is 15 ÷ 4 or 3.75–1 for a place.

Even this is something of an illusion however. As was shown on pages 12–14, the over-round in handicaps with very big fields is invariably much higher than elsewhere. The bookmaker is able to conceal his high percentage 'take' on the totality of the field because he can chalk up most of the runners at apparently big prices which, in reality, are far less generous than they look.

Therefore only bet each-way sparingly. If you particularly fancy the chances of a horse and wish to insure yourself against a near-miss, that is one thing. But betting each-way as a matter of policy on all or most selections will put money in the bookmaker's pocket in the long run.

4. Back Fancied Horses with a Bookmaker, Outsiders on the Tote

An arbitrary rule but a good one is never to back a horse on the Tote which is priced at 9–1 or less by the bookies. The Tote price will hardly ever beat that set by the bookmakers, and when it comes to favourites, virtually never. But the reverse is very much the case with winners at 10–1 plus, especially in very big fields.

Most people know all this, but few seem willing to change their habitual betting medium to fit circumstances.

Even if your preference if for the 'nanny', the Tote place pool is a mug's game. The Tote's 'take' from the pool is very high, and returns to long-suffering patrons of it paltry.

By contrast, the Placepot often gives real value in relation to starting prices. It is a sound bet, although seldom as easy as it looks.

5. Do Not Bet 'First Show', Especially on the Racecourse
The first set of prices each bookmaker chalks up on his board are not a serious proposition for the punter. Their object is to test the water and ensure that a layer does not 'catch cold' *vis-a-vis* his rivals by over-pricing a horse. Because of this, all very early prices are uniformly low, and ridiculously so for the favourite. Prices will lengthen and only an idiot bets before a proper market has formed.

Satellite prices in the betting shops come later, and their first show is more realistic. Even so it usually pays to wait.

If, on the other hand, it is known that a horse will be the medium of a genuine gamble, then one must get in early before the price shortens. Not many of us are often in this fortunate position however – fortunate, that is, if the gamble is landed.

6. Treat So-Called 'Information' with the Caution it Deserves
Racing insiders sometimes have access to knowledge which can be of immense value in a betting sense, but for obvious reasons they are not given to telling the world about it.

Talk to enough of the dolly-mixture of ordinary racegoers on the other hand and you can get a tip for every horse on the card. You will probably also get the name of the Derby winner in three years' time, even if it has not yet been foaled!

As for commercial tipsters, forget them. They deal in greed, fantasy and shoddy goods. But, a word from the right quarter that your fancy is fit and well and definitely 'off' today is worth its weight in gold, especially when the 'right quarter' has a definite stable connection.

7. Avoid 'Clues' When Reading Form
Most punters have a favourite indicator which they swear by as an aid to finding winners. Beaten favourites, course and distance winners, top weights in nursery handicaps,

the outsider in a three-horse race, horses priced at 9–1, last horse in the betting forecast each-way, first five-year-old from the eight stone mark downwards in handicaps, most recently placed runner in the field, horses which have travelled over 200 miles to race – these are just a few of the less fanciful.

Many such clues form a part of horse-gambling lore but, although they may pinpoint a winner from time to time, followed consistently over a period they are all certain losers. Racing is just not as simple as that.

8. Following Jockeys' Mounts is the Road to Ruin

Some people never learn, but if you indulge in this practice long enough, you will go broke in the end. Top jockeys may well be 'the punters' friend' and will often come up with a winner or two, but they also ride a huge percentage of losers (around 80 per cent), and hardly ever show a level stakes, seasonal profit on all their mounts.

On the other hand the human factor is almost as important in racing as the equine. As we saw in an earlier chapter, trainers' methods are well worth close study. Selective betting on runners from the right stable can be a paying game.

9. Where One of the Dubai Sheikhs has Two Runners in a Race, Always Prefer the First Colours over the Second

The men of the ruling house of Dubai are as honest as the desert night is long when it comes to racing their thoroughbreds. Whatever the stabling arrangements, whatever the press say, whatever the racecourse betting, if one of their horses is carrying the first colours with a second runner in the race, it is a near-certainty that the former will beat the latter.

Racing dailies as well as racecards give first colours in their programmes; the first colours for the 'big four' are:

SHEIKH MOHAMMED	– Maroon, white sleeves, **maroon cap, white star**
HAMDAN AL MAKTOUM	– Royal blue, white epaulettes, **striped cap**
MAKTOUM AL MAKTOUM	– Royal blue, white chevron, **light blue cap**
GODOLPHIN	– Royal blue, **royal blue cap**

Jockey's caps are the mark of distinction in determining the first colours, second colours have a different colour cap.

10. Adjust Stakes According to the Time of the Year

Reduce your Flat stakes drastically or stop betting altogether as soon as the rains come in September or early October. The transition from fast to soft ground plays havoc with form. Also, huge fields are a feature of the autumn on the Flat with so many animals running for their winter corn. There is no point in sacrificing a seasonal profit on the altar of a series of risky bets at this time of the year. Likewise, go very easy on the Flat in March and April. Form has yet to settle down.

With jumpers, form before Christmas is generally overturned afterwards as the better class animals near their peak, putting early types in the shade. Concentrate on firm ground specialists up to September, but October and November are similar to March and April on the Flat.

11. Don't Bet Just for the Sake of Betting

Having a bet just for fun and interest is a different matter, but if profit is your main motive, wait for it. The right horses in the right races will come if you have patience.

12. Never, Ever Bet More Than You Can Afford to Lose

The golden rule *par excellence* of all gambling, for totally obvious reasons. 'Don't chase your losses' is another racing maxim that should *never* be forgotten.

9
Bet with Method and Win

'Bet with method and WIN!' was the sales slogan of a betting magazine for which the author used to write in the 1960s and 1970s and which featured regular contributions from many of the best racing brains in the country at that time. The *Sporting Investor* is now, sadly, long defunct but its message lives on. Random betting does not pay; a methodical approach based on form and statistics gives the punter a fair chance of winning consistently.

The right psychology when it comes to betting is also an essential, without which nothing can be achieved. Perhaps the biggest single reason why most ordinary racing enthusiasts ultimately fail in their attempts to 'beat the book' is that they expect too much from their financial interest in racing. No sensible person would expect to thrive overnight in a commerical enterprise with just a small amount of capital invested. Why then do so many people, knowing full well the risks attached to backing horses, live in the constant hope of amassing a huge sum, for just a few pounds, in double-quick time?

The facile glamour which surrounds the 'Sport of Kings' may have much to do with it. Racing has always exuded an aura of apparently easy money which even the most hard-headed enthusiast finds difficult to resist, at least in the first instance. If racing is an activity where a lot of very rich men and women are prepared to spend thousands, even millions, for the pleasure of having their horses compete against one another, surely, the tyro says to himself, it is not unreasonable to suppose that just a little of this excess of wealth will rub off on anyone who is willing to spend some time in the serious study of the finer points of the sport.

However, racing is a hard school for all concerned and not least for those who bet on it. The favourite you backed, incredibly, finishes plumb last. An outsider which carries your cash is beaten in a photo finish. Very soon the dreams of easy pickings fade as fast as the winning burst of the 'certainty' in the big race you meant to back, but for some unaccountable reason did not. Racing is full of what might have been, for to err is human, and the sport has a way of extracting high penalties for the slightest mistake, or error of judgement.

As they learn more about the game, most level-headed people, whilst their enthusiasm remains undiminished in many cases, come to realise that racing is in fact a pastime, not the royal road to instant riches. Yet if horse racing is a hobby or a diversion, a 'great triviality' in a famous phrase, that does not mean it cannot, within reason, be a profitable one. The irrational hopes of vast wins for virtually nothing will almost certainly prove elusive, but this is not an argument that betting should not be organised along sound, businesslike lines.

A handsome payout from a limited outlay may be achievable from time to time, but any betting venture, even the most speculative, needs to be carefully planned, not merely in the context of a single day's racing, but in terms of a fairly prolonged series of wagers which may extend over an entire racing season or perhaps even longer.

There are four key elements in devising a winning strategy:

1 A sound method of selection or, more likely, several sound methods for different phases of the racing year, all ultimately working together towards the goal of a long-term profit.

2 A sensible method of staking either on single or

multiple bets and, also, the willingness to take profits at appropriate times. No one can go on winning for ever, and 'giving winnings back to the bookie' is one of the worst failings of many punters.

3 An adequate betting bank that will see the punter comfortably to the end of a period of betting and afford the time and financial breathing space necessary to allow sound practice to pay off. Just as important, the betting bank should be sufficient to get the backer through those times when the going gets particularly tough. Here it generally pays to budget for the worst possible scenario.

4 The ability to learn from past mistakes and to modify betting procedures with a view to eliminating them in the future. In this a complete record of all bets struck is a most valuable aid. Such a record will help to establish which parts of a betting operation are suspect or just not working. It will also eradicate the gambler's trap of a dream world where a few wins are thought to compensate for many conveniently forgotten losses, thus masking a substantial deficit in the long term.

Backing horses, therefore, should never be regarded as a matter of pure chance, for much can be done to eliminate the element of luck in betting. The hit-and-miss punter who makes no plan and who simply hopes for the best will nearly always lose, and sooner rather than later. Anyone who is prepared to harness one or more of the formulae set out in this book to a controlled betting strategy must have reasonable prospects of making his pastime pay. Bookmakers treat horse racing as a business. So should you.

INDEX

group betting 63–73

Hamilton 93
handicaps/non-handicaps
 and classic system 103
 forecasts 83, 84
 and form 84–7
 form figures 78–9
 jumpers 115
 race ratings 76–7, 77
Hannam, Charles 63
Hannon, Richard 92

inside information 120

jockeys 86
 caps 122
 mounts 121
judgement 109
jumpers, form plan 115

level stakes 10, 33–4
Lincoln 70
losing runs 10, 21, 26, 35

market 12, 13–14, 68, 80, 120
mathematical probability 13–14
mutuel odds (America) 17

National Hunt
 and '28-day-rule' 89–90, 115
 Cheltenham/Kempton plan
  106–9
 forecasts 82, 83
 and form figures 79–80
 and trainer form 91
nervous energy 87–8
Newmarket 96–8, 99, 101–2
newspapers
 forecasts 12, 80
 race ratings 76–7
Newton Abbott 110

odds
 bookmakers' percentages
  12–14, 63–73
 bookmakers' system 63

influencing stakes 11
 over-round 14, 16, 65–6
 odds-on 117–18
 overlay system (America) 17–18

permutations 37–8
 accumulators 37, 43–7, 49
 compound perms 43–5
 doubles 37, 38
 fourfolds 43–7
 guarantees 39, 40, 41, 42, 44,
  45
 reduction plans 38–43, 49
 trebles 37
Placepot 119
Pontefract 93
psychology of betting 10, 123–4

race ratings, newspapers 76–7
Redcar 93
risk element 37, 73
Royal Hunt Cup 70

Salisbury 93
Sandown 93, 101–2
Sedgefield 110
selection strategy 75–93
 see also form
size of field 15–16, 85, 92–3, 114
Sprint Championship 98, 101–4
sprints 86, 92, 114
staking plans 21–35, 95, 124–5
 cover-to-win system 24–8, 35
 graduated stake systems 21–4
 reverse Labouchère system
  28–33
 see also permutations; systems
Stoute, Michael 92
strategy, key elements 124–5
successful run 10
systems
 automatic 103, 106, 116
 Cheltenham/Kempton plan
  106–9
 for classics 95–8
 doubles plans 111–13, 114–15
 for four-year-olds 104–6

for late summer 109–111
'system that always wins' 95–8
top weights plan 114
see also staking plans
Thirsk 93, 110
three-mile chases, doubles plan
114–5
time of year, favourable 109, 110,
115, 122
tipsters 120
top weights plan 114
Tote prices 18, 119
trainer form 92
'tuning up' 85

value
in the odds 12, 14, 16–17, 63
systems 17–18
variable stakes 9–11

weight 84, 114
weight-for-age scale 76

Yankee 45
Yarmouth 110
York 93, 99–100, 101, 110